Southern Branch Lines

MICHAEL WELCH

In association with members of the GLO

Capital Transport

ISBN 1 85414 306 9

Published by
Capital Transport Publishing
P.O. Box 250, Harrow, HA3 5ZH

Printed by
CT Printing Ltd, China

Front cover: Down in the woods, something puffed! Of all the branch lines covered in this volume, it was, perhaps, the Axminster to Lyme Regis line which was the best known. It had a strong identity all of its own, largely due to use of three Adams 4-4-2Ts which were retained especially to work this line long after the other members of the class had been pensioned off. They were ideally suited to the steep climbs and very sharp curves which characterised the route, as portrayed in this illustration of No.30583 puffing along sedately between Axminster and Combpyne in 1960. *JT*

Back cover: Grange Road station, on the Three Bridges to Tunbridge Wells line. If ever a rural station encapsulated the branch line age this was it! The train is a Tunbridge Wells-bound working, SECR H Class 0-4-4T No.31263 in charge. *GH*

Title page: 'It pays to take a cheap trip by train', according to the red poster on the waiting room wall. This was the scene at Bere Alston station at about noon on Sunday 13th September 1959. Ivatt 2-6-2T No.41317 sits in the up loop platform after arrival with the 11.12am from Callington. *JL*

Introduction

Allhallows, Bexhill West and Callington ... it almost seems as if the Southern Railway had a branch line for every letter of the alphabet. Certainly, when the network of branch lines in the south of England was at its zenith in the mid-1920s, following the opening of the Fawley and Torrington to Halwill Junction lines, virtually every town of any consequence in the region had a rail connection.

The first public, steam powered passenger and goods railway to be opened in the south of England was that between Canterbury and Whitstable in Kent, and this opened as early as 3rd May 1830. This 6-mile long line, of purely local importance, was built primarily to convey goods from Canterbury to the small port Whitstable. This line was physically isolated from the rest of the system at first, but became a branch from Canterbury West station when the Ashford to Ramsgate line opened in 1846. So, perhaps this line has a just claim to be the oldest branch in the south of England outside the London area. The network of lines in the south of England, as in other parts of the country, grew because local people wished to see their own town linked to the railway system which was rapidly expanding in the middle of the nineteenth century. A survey of the routes featured in this book indicates that a peak of new lines was reached in the 1860s during the 'railway mania' years. Construction continued, albeit in much more modest numbers, right through to the end of the century and even into the twentieth century. The last line to be added to the map was the ill-fated Allhallows branch which was opened in 1932. So, in the south of England the period of branch line construction actually lasted more than a century! Sadly, by the time the last branch had been opened, the first closure had already taken place, some of the first casualties being short, obscure lines in the Portsmouth area, such as the Gosport to Stokes Bay line, closed in 1915, and the East Southsea branch. A fair number of closures occurred in the 1930s as bus competition started to reduce passenger numbers, the Bishops Waltham and Kemp Town branches, plus Ringwood to Christchurch and Chichester to Midhurst lines, all falling victim during this period.

Most of the branch lines in the south of England were constructed for the reason outlined above, but the justification for the building some of others was entirely different, while one or two lines actually began life as a tramway for the conveyance of minerals. The lines mentioned at the start of this introduction exemplify the diverse origins and character of the routes portrayed in this album. The branch from Stoke Junction, on the line from Gravesend to Port Victoria, to Allhallows-on-Sea, for example, was built in 1932 by the Southern Railway purely as (what might be called today) a 'business venture'. They wanted to promote Allhallows as a seaside resort to rival those already well established on the North Kent coast, but they had been rather over-optimistic and their plans failed completely with the result that Allhallows never grew beyond the status of a small seaside village with a hotel and a few caravan sites. For the vast majority of holiday-makers Allhallows-on-Sea remained very much a 'last resort'. The short 4½-mile long branch from Crowhurst, on the London to Hastings route, was built for entirely different reasons. There was considerable traffic to and from the fashionable and elegant town of Bexhill-on-Sea which was monopolised by the London, Brighton & South Coast Railway (LBSCR). The South Eastern & Chatham Railway's (SECR) line passed within a few miles of Bexhill, so the company decided to construct a branch in order to gain a share of this lucrative business. The venture was sanctioned in 1897, but opening to a new terminus called Bexhill West did not take place until 1st June 1902. Through trains on the SECR route bettered those on the rival LBSCR line by 21 minutes, but much of its advantage was lost when the (former) LBSCR route was electrified in 1935. The number of through trains on the SECR route was subsequently reduced and these services were withdrawn altogether when the Second World War broke out. Traffic slowly dwindled and the line was closed in June 1964 despite the introduction of a frequent diesel service in 1958. The origins of the Callington branch, on the Devon/Cornwall border, could not have been more different. For many years the area around the town had been a hive of mining activity, but poor transport links prevented expansion. On 7th May 1872 the East Cornwall Mineral Railway (ECMR) opened a 7¾-mile long 3ft 6in-gauge line from Kelly Bray, near Callington, to Calstock Quay on the river Tamar. This involved the installation of a cable-operated incline from the quay to a point 350ft higher on the hillside above the valley, where wagons joined the main part of the tramway. In 1891 the line was taken over by the Plymouth, Devonport & South Western Junction Railway (PDSWJR) which had been recently opened its nearby line from Lydford to Devonport, but it was not until 1900 that a Light Railway Order was obtained to enable conversion of the ECMR to a standard gauge passenger-carrying line to link up with the PDSWJR 'main line' at Bere Alston. Before this could be achieved a huge viaduct had to be constructed at Calstock across the river Tamar and after its completion the branch was opened to passenger traffic on 2nd March 1908.

Sadly, the branch line age in the south of England outside the London area is over, with a few, very few, notable exceptions. After the closures before the Second World War already mentioned, more and more 'last days' occurred in the 1950s as passengers drifted away from the railways. But worse was yet to come, and in the 1960s, it was the unrelenting growth in private motoring, coupled with very short-term political decisions by governments of both major parties, that sealed the fate of many lines right across the network. It is to be regretted that British Railways did so little to promote the lines and make economies, which might have saved some from the late Doctor (later Lord) Beeching's dreadful axe. I hope the pages that follow convey at least some of the charm, character and remarkably relaxed atmosphere of the network of branch lines in the south of England shortly before many of them were swept away for ever. Opinions will differ whether some of the lines featured in this album should be classed as branch lines or secondary routes. Some of the lines included were originally secondary routes that were subsequently reduced in status as a result of closures, the 'branch' from Hurst Green Junction to Uckfield being a classic example.

I would like to thank all of the members of the GLO who kindly trusted me with their irreplaceable transparencies for publication in this album. Special thanks are also due to Chris Evans, David Fakes, John Langford and Graham Mallinson who read the proof and suggested a host of corrections and improvements to the text. Edwin Wilmshurst also assisted in a variety of ways and thanks are also due to this gentleman. I accept full responsibility for any errors that remain.

Burgess Hill, West Sussex, August 2006   MICHAEL WELCH

Contents

It is, perhaps, unfortunate that the first branch line to be featured in this album is totally untypical of those illustrated in the rest of the book. This is because the Folkestone Harbour branch was built to cater solely for boat train traffic and not to provide passenger and goods services to the local community. The South Eastern Railway (SER) bought the harbour way back in 1843 and opened the branch to passenger traffic six years later. Improvements to the harbour in 1885 enabled an advertised timetable of sailings to be introduced regardless of the tides. In times gone by there was a very substantial layout at Folkestone Harbour station which extended along the pier towards the lighthouse. There was a bank of thirteen sidings and a goods warehouse east of the station while, on the western side, there were many carriage sidings located between the seashore and Marine Parade. In both cases access could only be gained by running through the station and along the pier, before reversing into the yards. In BR days the railway installations at Folkestone Harbour were steadily reduced, goods traffic being finally withdrawn in August 1968. In this view, taken on 18th September 1959, an unidentified former Western Region (WR) pannier tank locomotive can be seen just beyond the station platforms. Surprisingly, perhaps, the third rail is already in place for the forthcoming electrification, the platform on the right extended and lifting barriers installed. *GD*

FOLKESTONE HARBOUR BRANCH

After crossing an access road to the station, just beyond the Harbour station's platforms, the railway line crosses over part of the harbour on a swing bridge, some of which is just visible on the right of this shot. The bridge separates the inner harbour (on the left) from the outer harbour. The line is carried over the rest of the harbour's waters on a series of brick arches which mark the start of the famous and extremely challenging 1 in 30 climb up to Folkestone Junction, one of the steepest gradients in the country. During the climb the line passes through an ordinary residential suburb of Folkestone and is bordered on both sides by attractive houses, the windows of which must have rattled noisily every time a train pounded up the bank at little more than walking pace. One wonders how housewives reacted on washing day to the clouds of black smoke being emitted by the locomotives as they staggered up the incline. In this photograph, taken on 20th September 1959, an unidentified pannier tank engine is seen pushing hard at the rear of a boat train ascending the bank. Note the quite remarkable variety of coaching stock forming the train, which includes two Pullman cars and BR Standard Mk.1 vehicles in addition to various carriages of Southern Railway origin. *JL*

For many years the boat trains to and from Folkestone Harbour were powered by R1 Class 0-6-0Ts which were rebuilds of the R Class engines originally built for the South Eastern Railway between 1888 and 1898. On occasions as many as four of these locomotives could be seen charging up the bank on one train! In March 1959 they were replaced by Great Western Railway (GWR)-designed pannier tank engines and the R1s became redundant. In this picture Nos.31128, 31047, 31010 and 31107 present a melancholy sight at Folkestone Junction shed on 30th March 1959. The odd one is No.31010 which had been modified for use on the Canterbury & Whitstable line where there were restricted clearances. *JL*

The New Romney branch's bleak and featureless landscape, not to mention the early dieselisation of its passenger services, did little to entice railway photographers and consequently few transparencies of this relatively little-known line were submitted for this album. The passenger service from Appledore, on the Hastings to Ashford line, to Dungeness was inaugurated on 1st April 1883, the branch from Lydd (later Lydd Town) to New Romney opening on 19th June 1884. In the 1930s land was given to the Southern Railway in order to promote holiday camp and bungalow projects along the seashore and the New Romney line was re-routed to serve them. This more circuitous route included two new stations and joined the original line about three-quarters of a mile short of New Romney station. One of the new stations, Lydd-on-Sea, was considered adequate to serve the needs of Dungeness, the station there being closed from 4th July 1937 when the new line became operational. The line had many level crossings, there were fourteen between Appledore and Lydd Town alone, which had picturesque names such as Tillery, Fielders, Mountain and Coldharbour. At one time there was considerable shingle traffic to the Potteries, but today just the freight-only line to Dungeness nuclear power station survives, the rest of the route having succumbed to closure on 6th March 1967. In this illustration South Eastern & Chatham Railway C Class locomotive No.31218, which was built at Ashford Works in December 1900, poses at Lydd Town station with a goods working on 7th June 1961. *GD*

The Southern Railway was always an optimistic and enterprising company, but its hopes were not always realised and they were certainly dashed in the case of the Allhallows branch whose principal claim to fame is its very short existence. The branch was an offshoot of the Gravesend to Port Victoria line, which itself had a chequered history, the latter opening throughout on 11th September 1882. The SER had ambitious plans to develop Port Victoria, but despite their best efforts and those of their successors, insufficient traffic was attracted to make the port viable and the line beyond Grain was closed on 11th June 1951. During the 1930s an attempt was made to develop Allhallows-on-Sea as a seaside resort and a 1¾-mile long branch was opened 14th May 1932 from Stoke Junction on the Port Victoria line. But the place never developed much beyond a camping and caravan site, to which many visitors arrived by car, and traffic, which had always been light, was insufficient to justify the line's existence. Passenger trains on the entire branch ran for the last time on 3rd December 1961, but freight workings to an oil terminal at Grain continue. Here H Class 0-4-4T No.31553 poses at Allhallows with a train to Gravesend on 17th June 1960. *RD*

Steam locomotives require to be 'coaled' and 'watered' regularly and the railway timetable had to allow time for their essential needs. Tank locomotives, in particular, had only a limited water supply which needed frequent replenishment. In this picture, which was taken on the same day as the previous illustration, No.31553 has moved up the platform to take water prior to returning to Gravesend and the crew can be seen carrying out this routine operation. Note the emptiness of the station's surroundings with only caravans visible, providing ample testimony of the Southern Railway's total failure to transform Allhallows into a premier Kentish resort! *RD*

Oast houses, hop gardens, apple orchards, lovingly maintained stations with a charm of their own, few routes could beat the Hawkhurst branch's scenic delights and relaxed, unhurried atmosphere. Several attempts were made to bring rail transport to this area of the High Weald of Kent before the SER opened a branch from Paddock Wood to Hope Mill (later Goudhurst) in 1892. In September 1893 an extension to Hawkhurst was brought into use. The line negotiated a series of parallel ridges separated by deep valleys and consequently there were some fierce climbs, such as the 1 in 60 facing southbound trains between Goudhurst and Cranbrook. The route was famous for hop-pickers' specials which brought trainloads of Londoners down from the Capital, but these workings steadily declined in the 1950s. Unfortunately, the line suffered from the classic drawback of so many branch lines, because most stations were some distance from the settlements they were supposed to serve. Travellers arriving at Goudhurst station, for example, were probably dismayed to find the village was a mile away up a hill that involved a 300 foot climb!
H Class No.31500 is depicted on 6th May 1961 at a damp Horsmonden station with a Hawkhurst-bound train. *RD*

A picture of Goudhurst showing H Class No.31177 propelling a Paddock Wood-bound train out of the station on a rather overcast 5th June 1961. The station here was fully equipped with a signalled passing loop and two platforms, so it was possible to cross passenger trains at this point. The tall, slender building that is the stationmaster's house, which adjoins the main station building, is prominent. There was a two-road goods yard on the up side, out of the shot. Note the enthusiasts at the far end of the down platform, no doubt braced to photograph the train as it pulled out. *GH*

Cranbrook was the largest intermediate centre of population on the Hawkhurst branch, so it was particularly unfortunate that the town was almost two miles away from the station! The line's inconveniently sited stations were probably a large factor in its downfall, closure occurring from 12th June 1961, before the late Doctor (later Lord) Beeching started to wield his infamous axe. The Locomotive Club of Great Britain arranged a 'last day' rail tour and in this illustration the train is seen leaving Cranbrook during a summer downpour. The locomotives are O1 Class No.31065 and C Class No.31592, both of which are based on the Bluebell Railway, though the latter is not operational at the time of writing. *GD*

A view of the lovely rural station at Cranbrook, taken on 20th June 1961, just over a week after closure. Note that the signalbox nameboard and station signs have already been removed to deter souvenir hunters, but the signal arms are still in position. The stationmaster's house appears to be of a similar design to that at Goudhurst, while the unpretentious station building is like other stations on the line and consists of a simple single-storey building of corrugated iron with a short wooden platform awning. Half a mile beyond Cranbrook trains passed through Badger's Oak tunnel (178yds) which was the summit of the line where it crossed the main watershed of the Weald. *GD*

At first sight Cranbrook station goods yard seems to have a prosperous air in this picture with a C Class 0-6-0 busily engaged on shunting the yard and two men apparently filling sacks of coal, while two other gentlemen, one of whom is obviously a railwayman, are conversing at the end of the platform. But, unfortunately, this shot is very deceptive because it was also taken on 20th June 1961 after all services had been withdrawn (as evidenced by the blank nameboard) and the train was being run in connection with the demolition of the line or, perhaps, to clear wagons. Note the rather dainty shunt signal on the left. *GD*

A further illustration of the LCGB's 'South Eastern Limited' rail tour on 11th June 1961, this time depicting the train at Hawkhurst station after the O1 locomotive had been detached. Hawkhurst was laid out as a through station to facilitate a projected extension to Rye but, almost needless to say, these plans came to nought. The large building on the left, as may be guessed from the smoke vents, was originally an engine shed, which was taken out of use in the early 1930s. Latterly the service consisted of half a dozen trains on weekdays only. On the freight side there was some coal traffic plus pot plants and flowers, but these were insufficient to sustain the line in the long-term and when the movement of schoolchildren was transferred to the local bus company in about 1958 this was probably the final nail in the line's coffin. *GD*

PADDOCK WOOD TO HAWKHURST

The South Eastern Railway first obtained powers to construct a line along the Westerham Valley in the mid-1860s, but it was local landowners and traders who eventually secured the incorporation of the Westerham Valley Railway in July 1876. They were authorised to construct a 4¾-mile long branch from Dunton Green, on the Charing Cross to Tonbridge main line, to Westerham. An extension to join the LBSCR line at Oxted was also envisaged but the SER refused to co-operate and this part of the plan was abandoned. In June 1879 the promoters reached an agreement with the SER who undertook to manage and operate the Westerham branch and it eventually opened to traffic on 7th July 1881. The formation was built for a double track line, but only one track was laid. There was an original intermediate station at Brasted, to which the SECR added Chevening Halt, 1¼ miles from Dunton Green, in 1906. In this illustration SECR H Class 0-4-4T No.31518 is seen leaving Brasted on 26th July 1959. The photographer's activities appear to have been spotted by the children travelling in the front coach! *CG*

Photographed on 11th March 1961, this scene shows H Class tank
locomotive No.31551 taking water at Westerham. The coaches are
both Maunsell vehicles which have been formed into a permanent
set and adapted for push-pull operation. Note the rather splendid
vintage shunt signal on the right. No.31551, which dated from
1905, was lucky enough to be fitted with push-pull apparatus,
presumably during a heavy works overhaul, in September 1960
and this undoubted good fortune enabled the locomotive to
survive long after many of its sister engines had been withdrawn.
It lasted at Three Bridges shed until January 1964, when the last
three examples of this long-lived class were condemned. *GH*

DUNTON GREEN TO WESTERHAM

A further view of No.31551 at Westerham on 11th March 1961, this time showing part of the goods yard which appears to have been deserted on the day this shot was taken. The 15th of January 1957 was a day to remember, when Bulleid 'West Country' Pacific No.34017 *Ilfracombe* was an unprecedented sight on the branch, working a day excursion from Westerham to Kensington Olympia. Westerham probably suffered from its close proximity to Oxted, which provided a direct service to London, and declining patronage in the mid-1950s led to the withdrawal of many off-peak trains and the demotion of Brasted station to an unstaffed halt. After the branch's closure on 30th October 1961 local people planned to take over the line, but received little support from the authorities because part of the trackbed was earmarked for a road scheme. *GH*

Unlike most lines featured in this book, the principal purpose of the Bexhill West branch was to be a direct main line link; it was built to enable the SECR to tap the lucrative Bexhill traffic, which was monopolised by the London Brighton & South Coast Railway (LBSCR). The 4½-mile long line from Crowhurst was sanctioned in 1897, but construction was delayed by the very substantial earthworks required and the building of a seventeen-arch viaduct across Combe Haven Valley. The double track route took over four years to complete and it eventually opened on 1st June 1902. The SECR route shortened the distance to London by ten miles and the fastest trains by this route took 1hr 39min compared to the LBSCR's best trains which took two hours. The branch was provided with through services, but the electrification of the LBSCR route in 1935 undermined the position of the SECR line which lost some of its through trains and these ceased entirely when war broke out. For many years LBSCR D3 Class 0-4-4Ts were the mainstay of the line until they were replaced by SECR H Class tank engines, the latter giving way to DEMU operation from 9th June 1958. Despite this investment in new stock, not to mention a new hourly service providing connections with London trains at Crowhurst, passenger numbers continued to fall and the branch was closed to all traffic on 15th June 1964. This portrait of the station was taken on 14th March 1962. *GD*

This picture, which was taken on the same day as the previous photograph, shows the somewhat deserted scene at the buffer stop end of Platform 2. The platform canopy was of generous proportions and extended 400 feet along platform Nos. 1 and 2. Gas lighting was provided for the platforms, but the buildings were lit by electricity. Platform 3 is on the right of the picture, but it was overgrown and had apparently been steadily grassing over since the 1930s! Remarkably, this platform remained available for use, at least in theory, until the station's demise. The signal box in the middle of the picture, rather oddly located by the buffer stops, is Bexhill No.2. It was originally equipped with a 22-lever frame and controlled the crossover, but had been reduced in status to a ground frame as early as the First World War. The other signal box, located between the main running lines and the goods yard, was sizeable and housed a 123-lever frame. The main station building, which is quite ornate, still survives. *GD*

Photographed just a week before cessation of passenger services, 2-car 'Hampshire' DEMU No.1121 is seen at Sidley on 7th June 1964 with the 3.05pm Crowhurst to Bexhill West train. The station was situated in a cutting and 280,000 cubic yards of earth had to be excavated before construction could begin. A further 20,000 cubic yards had to be removed to make room for the goods yard and all of this spoil was taken by the contractors for further use at Bexhill. The principal station building at Sidley (a small part of which is just visible above the bushes on the right) was far too large for the meagre amount of traffic and in the late 1930s the Southern Railway moved the booking office to the up side waiting shelter, part of which was adapted for its new use. This enabled most of the substantial brick-built main structure to be let for commercial use. Incredibly, a very commodious goods shed was erected at Sidley despite its close proximity to Bexhill: there were clearly no limits to the optimism of railway companies at that time! It was never a feasible proposition and was sold out use in 1929. *RP*

In the author's opinion, by far the most attractive branch line in Sussex, and arguably one of the best covered by this book, is the outstanding Polegate to Eridge 'Cuckoo line'. The line had everything a railway enthusiast could wish for, splendid Wealden scenery, elegant well-kept stations and fearsome gradients that took the line up to almost 500 feet above sea level. Strangely, few pictures of this route were submitted for this album, perhaps because towards the end some of the services were operated by DEMUs, especially at week-ends. The short section from Polegate to Hailsham was opened in 1849 whilst the remainder of the line was brought into use in 1880. In this shot BR Standard Class 4MT 2-6-4T No.80089 is seen leaving Polegate with a train bound for Tunbridge Wells on 11th June 1965, just a few days prior to the line's sad demise as a through route on 14th June. During the final few days of steam working in the Eastbourne area some engines carried the driver's name chalked on the front of the locomotive, as seen here. A diesel shuttle service survived on the Polegate to Hailsham section for a further three years. The old Polegate station, seen in the background of this illustration, was later closed and new premises opened on a different site. Virtually everything of railway interest in this picture, apart from the main line tracks, has gone, including the very solid-looking signal box. The former station building survives as a public house and restaurant. *GH*

Apart from the attributes mentioned in the previous caption, the 'Cuckoo line' was also famous for the fact that four consecutive stations had names beginning with the letter 'H', namely Hailsham, Hellingly, Horam and Heathfield. In this photograph, taken on 4th June 1965, a rather dirty BR Standard Class 4MT, No.80141, is depicted at Horam with an unidentified Eastbourne-bound working. Known as Horeham Road for Waldron until 1891, the station's name was altered to Horeham Road & Waldron for the short period up to 1900. For the ensuing 35 years Waldron & Horeham Road was preferred, until this was abbreviated to just plain Horam in 1935. When the line was built no expense was spared and even this very modestly sized station was provided with two signal boxes, both of which were later replaced by a lever frame on the up platform. *CG*

A study of Rotherfield and Mark Cross station on 18th November 1961 looking towards Eridge. This substantially-built station was in a lovely, peaceful setting, surrounded by woodland and unspoilt, undulating countryside. Sadly, it was almost a mile from the village of Rotherfield and, even worse, was 160 feet above it, so passengers without transport were faced with a considerable climb. Perhaps many found Crowborough station, located about 1½ miles westwards, a more convenient proposition and none of these factors augured well for the future of Rotherfield station. Even so, at this time the station was still smartly kept and the goods wagons in the yard plus the apparently newly-installed electric lighting gave it a false air of prosperity. *RP*

It is, perhaps, questionable whether the Hurst Green to Tunbridge Wells West line qualifies for inclusion in a book about SR branch lines because when these pictures were taken in the early 1960s it was a fairly busy secondary route. It did at least start as a branch line, the section from Hurst Green to Edenbridge opening on 2nd January 1888, but Edenbridge was a terminus for only a very brief period, the connection between there and Ashurst Junction being opened on 1st October of the same year. Ashurst Junction was where the line from Edenbridge joined the East Grinstead to Tunbridge Wells route. This line had been opened by a local company, the East Grinstead, Groombridge and Tunbridge Wells Railway, on 1st October 1866. During the twilight years of steam traction BR Standard Class 4MT 2-6-4Ts were a familiar sight on the route and in this picture No.80094 takes the Edenbridge line at Hurst Green Junction in June 1962. That year saw many steam workings taken over by 3-car 'Oxted' DEMUs. Today only the Hurst Green to Uckfield and East Grinstead lines survive in this area, so Edenbridge Town station is, once again, on a branch line! *CG*

The author cannot recall seeing many photographs taken at Edenbridge Town in steam days and certainly shots in colour are not plentiful. In this illustration an extremely decrepit looking BR Standard Class 4MT 2-6-4T, No.80018, pauses with the 11.08am Victoria to Tunbridge Wells West train on 29th October 1961. The deplorable external condition of No.80018 was typical of much BR motive power at that time. Some sheds such as Brighton, however, managed to keep their engines nicely polished, perhaps because they were able to recruit engine cleaners, and consequently had an excellent reputation. Clearly, cleaners were in very short supply at Tunbridge Wells West shed, where No.80018 was allocated at the time of this picture. *JL*

The photographer obviously thought very highly of the scope offered by Edenbridge Town station and, indeed, it was neatly kept, with the nicely proportioned station buildings undoubtedly enhancing the scene and producing a balanced picture. When he returned on 25th November 1961, however, BR painters were in residence and stepladders littered the premises. Despite this SECR H Class 0-4-4T No.31543 still manages to create a very powerful picture, as it pulls out with the 9.04am Oxted to Tunbridge Wells West train. *JL*

Today Ashurst is an undistinguished wayside station on the long branch that wends its way down from Oxted (Hurst Green Junction) to Uckfield, all that remains of a once busy network of secondary and branch lines in this part of the Weald. Remarkably, at one time Ashurst was the point at which the 4.48pm Victoria to Brighton/Tunbridge Wells West business train was divided, this ritual being carried out on Monday to Friday evenings. Certainly, this was one train where passengers had to make sure they were travelling in the correct portion if they wanted to arrive home in time for dinner: boarding the wrong coach could have serious consequences! Here, on 31st May 1962, an unidentified Maunsell N Class 'Mogul' waits in the platform while the train is split, whilst another Maunsell 'Mogul', this time U1 Class No.31892, simmers in the adjacent siding. What a wonderful way to commute! *JL*

No.31892 blows off furiously as it awaits departure from Ashurst with the Tunbridge Wells West portion of the 4.48pm *ex*-Victoria on 31st May 1962. Note the primitive platform oil lamps that were still used for illumination at this time and the old wheelbarrow which has presumably been pressed into use while the staff were doing a spot of gardening. This scene has since altered beyond recognition due to the unrestrained growth of lineside vegetation during the ensuing years and mature trees now encroach close to the tracks. The station building has since disappeared, but at least the footbridge is still *in situ*, as a token reminder of times past. *JL*

The Lewes to Tunbridge Wells line opened on 3rd August 1868 and involved a long climb in both directions to a gable summit on which Crowborough, the principal intermediate station, is sited. Ten years later the LBSCR obtained powers for a single line spur between the Lewes route and the Hurst Green to Tunbridge Wells line, thus enabling through running from London to Uckfield and Heathfield. This spur was used only for locomotive storage for a time, but was later doubled and commissioned for regular traffic. The point at which it joined the Lewes line was named Birchden Junction, which was in a secluded, rural location where its tranquillity was only occasionally disturbed by passing trains! In this picture, which was apparently taken from the steps of Birchden Junction signal box, BR Standard Class 4MT No.80065 takes the Tunbridge Wells line with (what was nominally) the 10.55am Brighton to Tonbridge train on 22nd July 1961. Actually, on arrival at Tonbridge this train formed a through working to Reading, but it is most unlikely that many *bona fide* passengers from Brighton to Reading would have taken this circuitous route. One wonders how the ticket collector would have reacted to such behaviour! *CG*

Photographed on the same day as the previous
picture, Maunsell 'Schools' Class 4-4-0 No.30936
Cranleigh heads southwards past Birchden Junction
signal box with the 1.12pm Tonbridge to Brighton
train. These locomotives were very highly regarded by
enginemen who considered them to be very competent
performers, so it is a great shame that No.30936 is in
such deplorable external condition. Sadly, by the date
of this picture, these locomotives had been ousted
from their duties on the Hastings Line and were
relegated to secondary work as depicted here. *CG*

An ornate oil platform lamp at Rowfant, the post of which has been 'embellished' with a standard BR green 'sausage' sign. *GD*

The branch from Three Bridges, on the Brighton main line, to East Grinstead was proposed by local entrepreneurs who formed the East Grinstead Railway Company. The customary 'cutting of the first sod' ceremony took place on 22nd November 1853 and the line was opened for business on 9th July 1855 with one intermediate station at Rowfant. Grange Road station was brought into use later. This portrait of Rowfant station was taken on 21st February 1960 and this view is looking westwards towards Three Bridges: note the staggered crossing gates. Part of the line around Rowfant passed through the estate of a local landowner who gave the land to the railway company with the proviso that they constructed a suitably decorated station for his use. A loop, up platform and footbridge were added at the turn of the century. *CG*

Unlike Rowfant, Grange Road station had
only one platform at which former London
& South Western Railway (LSWR) M7
Class 0-4-4T No.30055 is seen standing
with a two-coach train on 21st February
1960. At the time of this picture houses
were being constructed adjacent to the
station but, regrettably, this development
did not stop the line from being closed in
January 1967. A small shopping parade
now adorns the station site. *CG*

Another illustration of Grange Road station in 1960, but this shot was taken in September by which time the house builders appear to have moved out, although the new occupants do not seem to have arrived. The sight and sound of vintage motive power and coaching stock on their local line would have been a real treat for them! Here, on 18th September 1960, an unidentified LSWR M7 Class 0-4-4T awaits departure with the 4.08pm Three Bridges to East Grinstead train which is comprised of former LBSCR push-pull set No.723. The modest station, once called 'Grange Road for Crawley Down and Turners Hill' (note the giant-sized running-in board), was opened in March 1860 and apparently underwent enlargement in the late-1870s, though cynics would say it could not have been enlarged very much! There were a couple of sidings here, which were laid beyond the platform on the right to serve a small brickworks. *GD*

Construction of the 1¼-mile long Kemp Town branch was prompted by housing development to the east of the old town of Brighton and it opened for traffic on the 2nd August 1869. It diverged from the Brighton to Lewes line at Kemp Town Junction, just beyond Ditchling Road tunnel, which is located just east of London Road station. It must have been an exceptionally expensive line to construct due to the very heavy engineering works involved because, in addition to Lewes Road and Hartington Road viaducts, which were of three and fourteen arches respectively, there was also a 1,024-yard long tunnel before Kemp Town station was reached. Regrettably, the line proved to be something of a white elephant, being unable to compete with a direct and frequent tram service to Brighton town centre. It was closed to passengers on 1st January 1933, a very early casualty, but remained open for freight traffic until 1971. In the early 1960s the daily goods working from Brighton was still operated by steam traction and, on 14th April

1962, motive power was provided by E4 Class 0-6-2T No.32503 which is seen here passing the site of the erstwhile Hartington Road Halt. The locomotive is in quite presentable condition because, even at this late stage in its history, Brighton shed still continued its long tradition of keeping even the most humble goods engine in clean condition. *LD*

A number of steam-hauled enthusiasts' tours visited the branch during its closing years and in this view Maunsell Q Class No.30530 is also depicted passing the site of Hartington Road Halt with a special train on 18th October 1964 with the rooftops of Brighton forming the backdrop. The halt at this location was only open for just over five years prior to the First World War so it is hardly surprising that no trace remains in this picture. *JP*

A seagull's eye view (or should it be a pigeon's?) of the Kemp Town goods depot, also taken on 14th April 1962, with No.32503 performing shunting duties. This shot clearly shows the main station building and former passenger platform. Judging by the fair number of wagons in the yard, traffic was still reasonably buoyant at this time. The stretch of water on the horizon will probably be familiar to most readers. *LD*

A scene at the Kemp Town terminus on 29th December 1962, showing Ivatt 2-6-2T No.41327 shivering at the buffer stops after arrival with the daily freight train. Despite being closed to passengers almost thirty years previously, the station building was still intact and remained in use as a goods office and residence. No.41327 was an exile from the London Midland Region (LMR), one of many of these engines that were made redundant by dieselisation and moved to the SR where they ousted old pre-grouping locomotives. This engine was based at Skipton prior to its transfer to Brighton. *GH*

Beauty and the beast! Country railway stations do not come much finer than this splendid example at Ardingly, which was photographed on 26th October 1963 during the final weekend of services. The Ardingly branch was opened on 3rd September 1883 and the LBSCR built this intermediate station to serve both the village and nearby college. The architect was the renowned Joseph Firbank who designed a number of magnificent stations for the 'Brighton' company. The solid-looking tall building on the right is the station house and adjacent ticket office which were located at road level. Unlike other Firbank-designed stations, the main building was never completely tile hung. The ticket office was connected to the platforms by a gallery, which is visible above the down platform building. Facilities at platform level were rather basic, the down platform having only an alcove-like waiting area without doors, so it must have been a draughty spot! The station's only really busy moments were the beginning and end of term at the public school. Perhaps the highlight of the station's career was on 17th October 1933 when 'Schools' Class locomotive No.917 *Ardingly* paid a visit. If Ardingly station is the beauty in this shot, the beast is without doubt '2 Hal' electric unit No.2624. This type was designed just before the Second World War and noted for its hard, uncomfortable seating and, latterly, drab painted interiors. *CG*

HAYWARDS HEATH TO HORSTED KEYNES

The LBSCR was authorised by Parliament to build a line between Shoreham-by-Sea and Horsham in 1858 which was opened in stages in 1861, the section from Shoreham to Partridge Green on 1st July, while the remainder as far as Christ's Hospital (Itchingfield Junction) was brought into use on 16th September. In the author's opinion this route never really caught the imagination of railway aficionados like the steeply graded Polegate to Tunbridge Wells 'Cuckoo line' or the charming Horsham to Guildford branch with its particularly beautiful little stations. Perhaps the Shoreham to Horsham route's status as a double track line and its comparatively unremarkable scenery detracted from that indefinable 'branch line atmosphere'. The first station after Shoreham was Bramber, which served a small village, and the premises here were attractive enough but were, unfortunately, sited adjacent to a main road, so its location could hardly be described as idyllic. The station was the only one on the branch with electric lighting, as seen here in this picture which was taken on 5th December 1965. *RD*

During the early years of the BR regime stations were painted in their regional colours: the Western Region, for example, covered virtually everything in brown paint while in Scotland light blue predominated. The Southern Region opted for green and cream and the former is certainly to the fore in this picture of a pair of stepladders 'posing' against a lamp standard at Partridge Green (appropriately!) in 1964. One or two areas of rather weather-beaten cream paint are also visible. In the early 1960s many small rural stations had much to interest railway enthusiasts and many were virtually unchanged since pre-Grouping days, apart from the colour scheme, of course. The Beeching Plan foreshadowed the closure of many delightful country stations and very often those that survived had their buildings swept away to save maintenance costs. *RD*

Smartly turned-out BR Standard Class 4MT 2-6-4T No.80152 makes an energetic departure from Partridge Green with a three-coach Brighton to Horsham train which is formed of a set of Maunsell coaches dating from 1936. This picture was taken on 9th May 1962, a lovely spring day. The station's modestly sized goods yard can be seen on the right of the shot, while the roof of the goods shed is visible above the train. It is likely, however, that by the date of this photograph the yard had been closed. *CG*

The town of East Grinstead is well known, but West Grinstead does not have such a high profile, being merely a hamlet a couple of miles or so north-west of Partridge Green. Even so, despite its rather meagre traffic potential a station was provided, but built over a mile away from West Grinstead, adjacent to the Haywards Heath to Petersfield road which later became one of the principal cross-country routes in the area. This was another very pleasant country station where the birdsong was only occasionally interrupted by the sound of trains. In this shot LMSR-designed Ivatt Class 2MT 2-6-2T No.41260 rolls into the station with a southbound working on 9th May 1962. There appears to be a train of civil engineer's wagons in the siding and there is evidence of recent track work. Doubtless the BR accountants made a special note of the cost in order to bolster the case for closure. *CG*

Southwater was yet another station on the Steyning line located adjacent to a main road, in this case the route from Worthing to Horsham (now the A24), which presumably had a bus service competing with the railway. No doubt the bus took passengers destined for Horsham right into the town centre whereas the train would have deposited them about half a mile away which was hardly an attractive proposition for shoppers with heavy bags. Unlike other stations on the branch, Southwater did not have a footbridge and this nicely balanced portrait of the premises, which dates from 26th March 1964, has apparently been taken from a foot crossing. This view includes the tiny goods shed, which is just visible beyond the station building on the right, and the really vintage LBSCR signal box. A brickworks, which brought much valuable freight traffic to the line, used to be situated south of the station, beyond the platform on the right of the shot. *CG*

A Brighton to Horsham train, formed of a 3-set of comfortable Bulleid coaches, leaves Southwater and passes a shallow cutting dotted with primroses. This picture was also taken on 26th March 1964. Motive power is provided by Ivatt Class 2MT 2-6-2T No.41230 in unlined BR black livery. This locomotive was formerly based at Widnes, in the north-west of England, and was reallocated to Brighton in December 1962 presumably after becoming 'surplus to requirements' on the LMR. Trains ran for the last time here on 6th March 1966, from which date the 'Linger and Die', as the Steyning line was known locally, was closed to all traffic, apart from a siding serving the cement works at Beeding, just north of Shoreham, but even this remnant has now gone. *JP*

The Horsham & Guildford Direct Railway was a grandiose name for a new railway line, but was proof, if any was needed, that sometimes the most impressive names were given to the least significant schemes. This 15½-mile long single line ran from Stammerham Junction (Christ's Hospital) to Peasmarsh Junction, 1¾ miles south of Guildford. In 1864 the local company sold its incomplete works to the LBSCR which ran its first services along the route on 2nd October 1865. Apart from the small town of Cranleigh, the line did not serve any centres of population, but at least there was some freight traffic from Baynards where fuller's earth was railed. The initial service consisted of four through trains each way daily on weekdays which had been increased to six trains by the time of closure in June 1965, so this gives some idea of the traffic potential. It is one of the very few branches in the county of Surrey to have been closed. There was seldom any through working to other routes, but latterly there was a sporadic, but quite interesting, summer Sunday excursion usually from Reading to Brighton that changed engines at Horsham. This Southern Railway platform sign was photographed at Christ's Hospital station on 29th May 1965, a few weeks before closure. The narrow gap between the two platforms is explained by the fact that the single running line was served by platforms on both sides. *CG*

In this view taken on 8th August 1959 an LSWR M7 Class 0-4-4T, No.30047, is seen at pretty Slinfold station. Remarkably, at one time there were two separate private sidings here, one serving a brickworks whilst the other was used by a timber company. Long after the withdrawal of freight facilities, and removal of the track, a small hand-crane survived in the goods yard as a poignant reminder of more prosperous times. *CG*

Baynards station was built to appease Lord Thurlow, the owner of Baynards Park, whose land the route's promoters wished to cross. The railway company obtained the land at a very reasonable cost and in return built a station solely to serve the estate. It would be an understatement to say that Baynards station was in a peaceful rural setting, because there were no other buildings in close proximity. Besides its tranquillity, Baynards was also famous as the location of many film sequences, perhaps the best known being BBC Television's *The Railway Children*, filmed in 1957. In this photograph, taken on 4th September 1960, the station has been disguised as 'Valleywood' and M7 Class No.30124 is seen standing in the platform during a pause in the filming of *The Horsemasters* which starred Tony Britton, Donald Pleasence and Millicent Martin. The film was released in 1961. The coaches are Maunsell-designed 3-set No.961 which was built in 1936. *CG*

In addition to its popularity with film producers, Baynards station was also justly famed for its absolutely magnificent displays of dahlias which were tended by the station staff during the lengthy periods between trains. The flowers became something of a local tourist attraction but, almost needless to say, the vast majority of visitors arrived by car. Perhaps they made a modest contribution by buying a platform ticket! Some of the displays can be seen in this view of an un-typically bustling Baynards station which depicts a ramblers' special train awaiting departure towards Guildford behind M7 Class No.30056 piloting Maunsell Q Class 0-6-0 No.30545. A local train to Horsham with another M7 Class in charge waits in the up platform. This picture was taken on 4th September 1960. *CG*

Cranleigh station's status as the most important intermediate
point on the Horsham to Guildford line was emphasised by the
fact that it was the only one with a footbridge, which is
prominent in this shot taken in mid-1965, just prior to closure.
During the line's twilight years services were monopolised by
LMSR-designed Ivatt 2-6-2Ts of the type seen here. There was a
fair-sized goods yard at Cranleigh that was equipped with a large
loading gantry, the main commodities handled being timber
(outwards), and coal for the local gasworks. The only other
significant source of freight traffic was Baynards from where, as
previously mentioned, fuller's earth was despatched. *JP*

Photographed against the background of the extremely weather-beaten remains of Petworth station, LBSCR E4 Class No.32470 pauses with the daily pick-up goods in March 1962. The first station on this site lasted only 30 years and was replaced in the early 1890s, the official opening apparently being performed by the Duke of Connaught who was staying at nearby Petworth House. The signal box, on the left, boasted an 18-lever frame and in the early years bore various enamel advertisements which were, of course, intended to catch the eye of waiting passengers. *JP*

Opposite: The history of railways serving Midhurst is quite complex, largely because the town was served by two separate companies and, for a time, by two separate stations. The first route to reach Midhurst was the LSWR line from Petersfield which opened for business on 1st September 1864. The LBSCR's line from Horsham had reached Petworth by October 1859, this being the first line in the area, as the present route along the Arun valley to the coast did not open until 1863. The Mid-Sussex & Midhurst Junction Railway was incorporated in August 1859 with the intention of pushing on westwards and the Petworth to Midhurst link was finally opened after much delay on 15th October 1866. This was operated by the LBSCR which built its own station in the town, the LSWR premises being almost a stone's throw from the 'Brighton' station across a minor country road. The Chichester & Midhurst Company started construction in 1865, but work proceeded slowly owing to financial problems and had ceased completely by 1868. The LBSCR took over in 1876, opening the route to traffic on 11th July 1881. This line was noteworthy for the flamboyant architecture of its stations, especially Singleton, the station for Goodwood racecourse, which had two island platforms. It was decided that the junction at Midhurst with the existing line would face towards Petworth and this necessitated the building of a new station which was, unfortunately, further away from the LSWR's premises. When the Southern Railway took over it decided to concentrate all services on the second LBSCR station. This became effective from 12th July 1925 when the LSWR station was closed. Here LBSCR E4 Class 0-6-2T No. 32469 is seen shunting at Petworth on 14th April 1960: the train crew seem to be posing for their picture. The emptiness of the countryside surrounding Petworth is apparent from this shot, the town being two miles away! *CG*

A further view of No.32469 taken on 14th April 1960. The location this time is Selham, a small hamlet with a few houses and pub, so traffic from there could never have been heavy. The station opened on 1st July 1872, some years after the line was brought into use. Amazingly, there used to be a signal box at Selham, but it was closed in 1933 and replaced by two ground frames. Like all of the stations on the line, Selham handled a lot of milk traffic and many consignments of chestnut fencing were also apparently despatched from there. Selham closed to goods traffic in May 1963. *CG*

PULBOROUGH TO MIDHURST

The former LBSCR Midhurst station is depicted in this shot which was taken in April 1960. This station was actually the second 'Brighton' station to be built in the town because, as previously mentioned, trains from Chichester were unable to use the first one due to the position of the junction. By the date of this photograph most of the premises had fallen into disrepair but, judging by the curtains flapping at an open upstairs window, at least the station house was still habitable. This fine building was razed after closure and a housing development sprang up on the site. Traffic on the Chichester line was always pitifully thin, except on Goodwood race days of course, and passenger services were withdrawn from 8th July 1935. Passenger trains between Pulborough and Petersfield last ran on 5th February 1955, but goods facilities were maintained at Midhurst until October 1964. Petworth was the last point to retain a rail service, goods trains continuing to operate until 20th May 1966. *CG*

A fascinating picture of the remaining infrastructure at Midhurst taken on 14th April 1960, with No.32469 just discernible shunting in the yard. The course of the line to Chichester is clearly visible going off to the left, whilst the track continuing straight ahead is that of the erstwhile route to Petersfield which still served a local brickworks at this time. The LBSCR engine shed used to stand in the foreground, on the right. The water tower was still in existence, however, and can be seen on the extreme right. The building with the prominent chimney, immediately behind the goods shed, is the old LSWR station. *CG*

Plans for a railway line connecting Alton and Winchester were first mooted in 1845 when the LSWR undertook a survey of the land between the towns, but nothing came of this and fifteen years elapsed before the scheme was revived by the Alton, Alresford & Winchester Railway Company (AA&WR). This company enjoyed considerable local and parliamentary support and it was no surprise when it obtained its Act on 28th June 1861. Construction commenced in 1863 and, despite the massive earthworks involved, notably some very deep cuttings, the line opened throughout on 2nd October 1865. By this time the AA&WR had changed its name to the Mid Hants Railway Company, which was swallowed up by the LSWR in 1884. Like so many branch lines the route started to suffer from road competition in the 1930s. This slow decline was partly reversed in 1957 when the line became one of the first SR routes to be dieselised. Photographs of BR steam workings over the route are hard to find largely as a result of its early conversion to diesel operation, the line having nothing to attract steam photographers, apart from the occasional rail tour. All of this changed in the mid-1960s, the Alton to Winchester line being regularly used as a diversionary route at weekends when the Bournemouth Line was closed for engineering works in connection with its electrification. In this picture, which was taken on 15th May 1966, the 8.55am Bournemouth Central to Waterloo train disturbs the calm of rural Ropley as it passes through behind Stanier Class 5MT No.45493. This engine was an extremely unusual sight on the line, its appearance being explained by the fact that the previous day's York to Poole train was rostered at that time for Class 5MT haulage and the engine was booked to stable on Bournemouth shed until the following Monday morning, so was available for special traffic duty if required. *GH*

In this illustration the 10.34am Bournemouth Central to Waterloo train is seen climbing through Itchen Abbas station, also on 15th May 1966. The station here, which was previously known as Itchen Abbotts, was undoubtedly the least patronised on the line, serving only the village of Itchen Abbas and the tiny hamlet of Avington. The station lost its signal box and passing loop in the early 1930s and the small goods yard, which consisted of only two sidings, was closed in 1962. Staff were withdrawn in 1965 following the introduction of conductor guards and through trains ran for the final time on this route in February 1973, when BR withdrew the service. The section between Alton and Alresford is, of course, preserved as the Mid Hants Railway. The locomotive in charge is Bulleid 'Battle of Britain' Pacific No.34059 *Sir Archibald Sinclair*, which is in presentably clean condition, complete with name and number plates. It must have been a rare treat for the photographer to see an engine in such a polished state and it is a pity that the machine is not emitting any smoke to add life to the shot – obviously the engine was being skilfully handled! No.34059 is preserved at the Bluebell Railway and, at the time of writing, is nearing the end of a long and painstaking restoration from a derelict condition. *GH*

Construction of the 4½-mile long line from Havant to Hayling Island was proposed by the Hayling Railway Company which obtained its Act of Parliament in July 1860. Unwisely, this independent company chose to route its line along the western shore of the island on an embankment which involved reclaiming part of the Langston Harbour mudflats, but they had not anticipated the erosion by the tide which carried away the spoil almost as fast as the contractor deposited it! This grave oversight almost resulted in the company's collapse, but the appointment of a new chairman, Mr Francis Fuller, in 1866 proved to be its salvation. His arrival on the scene sparked an immediate revival of interest in the scheme and, more importantly, he purchased land to the east of the existing alignment, so the line could be built on a more stable and suitable course. The branch eventually opened throughout on 17th July 1867. There was a severe weight restriction across Langston Bridge, the dainty LBSCR 'Terriers' being the only locomotives permitted to cross. Traffic on the line was seasonal, with an intensive service being provided for holiday-makers during the height of the summer, especially at weekends, but the line was very quiet during the winter. One wonders how many passengers were on board this train as it awaits departure from Havant behind No.32678 on a snowy day in early 1963. *JP*

HAVANT TO HAYLING ISLAND

A close up view of Langston Bridge's 30ft-wide opening span, photographed on 13th May 1961. The existence of navigation rights around Hayling Island meant that an opening span had to be provided; the girders were pivoted on a wrought iron cylinder and travelled round a roller path. The wheel gearing was operated manually. The signal box had seven levers, of which only four were used regularly. The box ceased to be manned full-time in about 1938 and those wishing to have the bridge opened were obliged to contact Havant station and arrange a mutually convenient occasion. Before the span could be opened the signal wire had to be disconnected by the signalman and a lengthman available to remove two sets of fishplates. There were also locking bolts which were interlocked with the railway signals that protected the span. The post on the left was used for raising the signals, flags by daytime and lights at night, for water-borne traffic. *GD*

The classic Hayling Island branch scene! Photographed against a sombre sky, a LBSCR 'Terrier', hauling three coaches, rumbles across Langston Bridge on 2nd November 1963, and creates a memorable silhouette. This was the last day of public services. *GD*

The last act on the Hayling Island line! Whilst 2nd November was the final day of timetabled passenger services – there were no Sunday trains by this time – the very last train was an LCGB rail tour which ran on the following day. This working is seen with 'Terrier' No.32636 (the oldest locomotive in BR service) at the head of the train glinting in the afternoon sunshine. Another engine of the same class, No.32670, assisted at the rear. The coach in the shot is the experimental glass-fibre bodied vehicle, No.S1000S, which was constructed on the underframe of a carriage damaged in the Lewisham collision of December 1957. *GD*

HAVANT TO HAYLING ISLAND

The Hayling Island branch, as previously stated, has always been the preserve of the sprightly LBSCR 'Terriers' and one of these diminutive locomotives, No.32661, is pictured at North Hayling with a down train. The small halt, which was located in a remote, windswept area on the island's western shore, is totally obscured by the train. In years gone by there was a siding here to cater for the local oyster traffic. Note the vehicles in the car park that adjoined the halt: one of them looks to be at least as ancient as No.32661! Railway enthusiasts with a special interest in station lighting would have found this branch particularly interesting because Langston station was kitted out with electric lighting, North Hayling only a single oil lamp whilst Hayling Island station had gas. This picture was taken on 22nd May 1961. *GH*

In addition to signals for warning vessels in Langston Harbour, the Hayling Island branch also had some fine railway signals of which this splendid LBSCR specimen at Hayling Island station is an example. The train approaching in the background is headed by No.32640. This picture was also taken on 22nd May 1961. *GH*

The end of the line! A general view of the modest terminus at Hayling Island, photographed on 22nd July 1963 with No.32670 in the station. The somewhat basic layout here consisted of the main platform with a loop, at which the train is standing, and a bay platform without run round facilities. There was also a small goods yard, served by a daily mixed train on weekdays only, complete with a goods shed, loading dock and cattle pens. The A1X Class 'Terriers' had very small coal bunkers, so perhaps the most important item in the goods yard, at least from the engine crews' point of view, was a small coaling stage. On busy days a 30-minute interval service was operated on the branch which required very slick operation and huge numbers of passengers were carried on these peak days. On August Bank Holiday 1962, for example, by the time all of the passengers had alighted from the third train of the day from Havant a total of 1,500 tickets had reportedly been collected. Closure of the branch was caused by the allegedly poor condition of Langston Bridge, which apparently needed repairs costing £400,000. *GH*

Hayling Island station appeared to be quite busy when this shot was taken on 16th May 1959; A1X Class No.32650 simmers in the platform prior to departure with the next train to Havant. Note the neatly maintained flower-beds and spare coach in the bay platform which could be quickly pressed into service to prevent overcrowding. The goods yard also appears to be doing good business judging by the number of wagons on view. When the line was closed in November 1963 all remaining A1X Class engines were withdrawn from service, but all were purchased for private preservation, including the example seen here. *GH*

The Isle of Wight railway system included such delightful backwaters as the Newport to Freshwater and Merstone to Ventnor West branches. These lines must have been totally uneconomic, however, and were closed in the early 1950s, with other lightly-used lines following a few years later. By the early 1960s only the routes from Ryde to Cowes/Ventnor remained and continued to be operated by ancient, but increasingly unreliable, LSWR O2 Class locomotives, and vintage carriages. Unlike on the mainland, where similar worn-out stock was being rapidly replaced, the island's geographical isolation created unique difficulties and various solutions were put forward to solve the island's developing motive power crisis. The government decided that the comparatively busy Ryde to Shanklin section had to be retained and this stretch was eventually electrified. In the meantime the O2s soldiered on, and the Isle of Wight became a place of pilgrimage for railway aficionados from all over Great Britain until steam traction on regular passenger services finally bowed out, with hundreds of mourners present, at the end of December 1966. There were originally two sheds on the island, one at Newport and another at Ryde St John's Road. Latterly, only the shed at Ryde was operational and in this view, taken on 26th June 1960, a quartet of O2 Class engines is seen lined up outside the shed building: one of them, No.W27, *Merstone*, still had a Drummond boiler. Note the neat and tidy state of the yard and cleanliness of the engines – no wonder enthusiasts loved to visit the Isle of Wight! *CG*

Ryde St John's Road station is the location for this portrait of No.W25, *Godshill*, leaving with a Ventnor train on 27th April 1959 and passing the fine bracket signal at the country end of the station. The motive power depot is on the left, whilst part of the works building is just visible on the right. The signal box, which has a 45-lever frame, was formerly located at Waterloo East. *CG*

RYDE TO VENTNOR (ISLE OF WIGHT)

A bird's-eye view of Ventnor station, the site of which was carved out of St Boniface Down, an area of high downland which rises to over 700ft above sea level. The station was 276ft above sea level, so reaching it from the promenade must have involved a strenuous walk which probably deterred all but the most persistent and determined travellers! The caves were apparently used by local coal merchants. The train is powered by O2 Class No.W14 *Fishbourne*. Note the crimson liveried full brake at the end of the far siding. *CG*

The Isle of Wight railway system proved, as previously mentioned, to be an irresistible attraction for railway enthusiasts from all over the country until steam's demise and the reason for this is immediately apparent from this illustration. In this everyday scene, photographed in the lovely setting of Ventnor station on 18th September 1965, the fireman of O2 Class No.W20 *Shanklin* is about to replenish the locomotive's tanks before running-round the train which is waiting in the platform. Ventnor station had an island platform, the canopy of which is clearly visible above the engine, and this was linked to the main platform by a portable wooden bridge. The telephone box, immaculate saloon car and well-preserved Southern Railway sign add to the charm of this picture. One can almost hear the raucous sound of sea birds circling overhead, smell the salty sea air and hear the rhythmic panting of the O2's Westinghouse brake pump. Happy days indeed! *RJ*

RYDE TO VENTNOR (ISLE OF WIGHT)

One of the few photographs in this album that can still be taken today! This section of line through Ashey is preserved by the Isle of Wight Steam Railway who also own No.W24 *Calbourne*, this being the only member of the O2 Class to survive in preservation. Amazingly, there used to be a racecourse at Ashey which, on a good day, apparently attracted up to 3,000 spectators. Sadly, the grandstand was wrecked by fire in the late 1920s which ended Ashey's career as a horse racing venue. The station building's elegant architectural style reflected the status of the local landowner and the building still survives at the time of writing, in use as a dwelling. Following ground movement, in 1961 the track here was slewed to use the (then) overgrown down platform which is visible on the right. There used to be a loop at Ashey, but this was reduced to a siding in the mid-1920s, whilst the lightly-used station became an unstaffed halt in 1953. This picture was taken on 11th September 1960. *RP*

A train to Cowes leaves Newport on a sunny 26th June 1960 behind O2 Class No.W16 *Ventnor*, in customary clean condition, hauling a wonderful rake of vintage carriages. Newport was the hub of the island's railway system, with lines fanning out to Ryde, Cowes, Freshwater and Ventnor West. There was even a direct route to Sandown. By the time of this picture, however, the town's status as a railway junction had been lost, following closure of all lines serving Newport, apart from the Ryde to Cowes route which lasted until February 1966. *CG*

RYDE TO COWES (ISLE OF WIGHT)

In the early 1800s the naval town of Portsmouth was heavily fortified against an invasion from Europe. Consequently, the Admiralty did not wish to see the fortifications breached and steadfastly resisted early attempts to link Portsmouth with the fast-developing railway system, so it was not surprising that the first line in the Portsmouth area was a branch from Bishopstoke (Eastleigh) to Gosport on the western side of Portsmouth Harbour. This line was also opposed by the Admiralty but, even so, it was opened on 29th November 1841. It got off to an inauspicious start when, five days later, there was a heavy earth fall in Fareham tunnel which resulted in the line being closed for some months. So, citizens of Portsmouth who wished to travel by train to London started their journey by taking a boat across the choppy waters of Portsmouth Harbour to Gosport, from where they continued by train via Bishopstoke. In June 1847 the LBSCR's line from Brighton opened, becoming the first line into Portsmouth, and in 1859 the first services to and from Waterloo ran along the Portsmouth Direct line. Following these developments, which concentrated services on the two main Portsmouth stations, the branch to Gosport gradually declined in importance and was eventually closed to passengers on 8th June 1953, but continued in use for freight purposes until 1969 when the line was cut back to Bedenham. In this picture, taken at Fareham on 11th July 1961, the Gosport line goes straight ahead while the Portsmouth route takes a very sharp curve to the left. Today, the course of the Gosport line is almost totally hidden by bushes and even the alignment of the main line tracks was altered some years ago when new bridges were installed across the main road. Westbound trains now use the outermost face of the platform on the right, while the middle platform is now a bay. *JL*

In the mid-nineteenth century the town of Gosport, which has extensive links to the Royal Navy, was a very important place which was reflected in Gosport station's extremely impressive terminal building. Built in Italian style, it was designed by Sir William Tite and boasted fine arches and an elegant colonnade comprising of fourteen bays. The structure, which was photographed on the same day as the previous shot, is reputed to have cost £11,000. It has listed building status and is still standing at the time of writing. In 1845 the branch was extended beyond Gosport station into the fortified Clarence Yard where another station was built for the exclusive use of the Royal Family who used it during their frequent visits to the Isle of Wight. *JL*

Maunsell 'Mogul' No.31808 simmers in the former station platform at Gosport prior to leaving with the 5.35pm freight to Fareham on 11th July 1961. There was a two-road brick-built engine shed at Gosport which dated from the opening of the line in 1841. The building was partially destroyed by an air attack during the Second World War and replaced by a single-road corrugated asbestos structure. There were various branches off the Gosport line including one to Stokes Bay, which at one time boasted regular sailings to the Isle of Wight, and another to Lee-on-the-Solent. It would be a considerable understatement to say that both were early casualties because the former lost its passenger trains in November 1915 whilst those on the latter survived until 1931. *JL*

The independent Andover & Redbridge Railway was promoted in 1858 and both the LSWR and GWR sought to acquire the company. The former was successful and opened the line, which was built on the course of the Andover canal, on 6th March 1865 as a single line. The route was doubled in 1885. Perhaps this line is best known as the route of the through Cheltenham to Southampton trains, which travelled via Swindon, Marlborough and Savernake before reaching Andover. This extremely sparse service was withdrawn in September 1961 when the line from Cheltenham was closed to passenger trains. The line south of Andover was largely dieselised in 1958 so consequently colour pictures of scheduled steam passenger trains are rare. This shot of Horsebridge station, looking towards Romsey, was taken on 6th September 1964. *RD*

Stockbridge station was north of Horsebridge and this view, also taken on 6th September 1964, is looking towards Andover. Initially, when the line opened, there were four trains on weekdays and by 1906 the service had increased to eleven on weekdays with two on Sundays. Three of the weekday trains ran to and from the north of England via the Midland & South Western Junction Railway (MSWJR) and two carried names. By the 1940s there were seven weekday trains with two on Sundays and this level of service continued until the introduction of a relatively frequent diesel service south of Andover in the late-1950s. Despite the improved frequency of trains the line's slow decline continued and all services were withdrawn from 7th September 1964, the day after this photograph was taken. *RD*

The four-mile long single track branch from Brockenhurst (Lymington Junction) was officially opened by the Lymington Railway Company on 12th July 1858. The town was the terminus of services to the Isle of Wight which the company hoped to develop, but the branch languished because the LSWR concentrated on Portsmouth. This situation started to change for the better in 1878 when the independent company was vested in the LSWR. The year 1884 proved to be the real turning point in the line's fortunes with the extension to the pier being opened on 1st May, followed two months later by the LSWR's acquisition of the ferry service to Yarmouth. Connections were greatly improved and traffic steadily increased. In 1938 the Southern Railway introduced one of the first 'drive on, drive off' ferry services at Lymington. Many years later the branch achieved a degree of fame as the last in the country with a steam-operated passenger service which lasted until 3rd April 1967. The former LSWR M7 Class 0-4-4Ts were the staple power on the branch trains for many years and in this typical scene No.30048 is depicted at Lymington Town on 12th October 1963. *LD*

The beautiful, intricate brickwork of Lymington Town station's frontage is an absolute joy to behold in this picture, also taken on 12th October 1963. The scene is completed by the display of three vintage vehicles! The building seen here, which dated from 19th September 1860, was the terminus of the branch until the opening of an extension to the Pier station on 1st May 1884. In 1986 restoration was carried out by BR in conjunction with local organisations. Most of the accommodation was let for commercial purposes, but at least a ticket office was retained. *LD*

The LMSR-designed Ivatt 2-6-2Ts and BR Standard 2-6-4Ts dominated the branch during the last days of steam and, at first sight, this picture could easily be mistaken for an everyday timetabled service train: only the people peering out of the windows suggest that it is a rail tour. The train is the LCGB's 'Hampshire Branch Lines Rail Tour' which, appropriately, had BR Standard Class 4MT No.80151 at the front, and Ivatt 2-6-2T No.41320 at the rear, when it traversed the Lymington branch on 9th April 1967. The train is seen running alongside the Lymington River between the Town and Pier stations. This unusual method of operation was used due to the lack of run-round facilities on the branch for a long formation. *GD*

The location of this picture is self-evident! A train to Brockenhurst, with M7 Class No.30048 in charge, awaits departure on 12th October 1963. Note the collection of platform barrows that were presumably used to transport passengers' luggage from the ferry to the train and *vice versa*. By the date of this picture most of the M7 Class engines employed on the branch were completely worn out and it was no doubt to the relief of the enginemen when they were replaced in June 1964. *LD*

The line from Brockenhurst to Wimborne was originally part of the Southampton & Dorchester Railway – the famous 'Castleman's Corkscrew' – which was promoted under the energetic leadership of Mr A.L. Castleman, a Wimborne solicitor. It had been hoped to continue beyond Dorchester and Castleman envisaged the line continuing to Exeter as a principal trunk route, but these plans were thwarted by the larger companies when Castleman became too dictatorial for their liking. The line's unofficial name stemmed from the fact that the line took a very circuitous route in order to serve various centres of population, such as Ringwood, which at that time was one of the largest towns in the area. Construction of the Southampton & Dorchester Railway started on 21st July 1845 and the line was opened for traffic on 1st June 1847. The isolated station of Holmsley, which was known as 'Christchurch Road' for a time, is seen here in this picture taken on 11th April 1964. *RP*

The importance of towns such as Ringwood and Wimborne faded as Bournemouth developed rapidly into one of the largest, and certainly most popular, seaside resorts in the country. The growth of Bournemouth was, of course, encouraged by the opening of the direct route from Waterloo via Sway in 1888. By the 1960s traffic on the Ringwood line was pitifully thin, as exemplified here by this short two-coach train, the 2.20pm Bournemouth West to Brockenhurst with BR Standard 2-6-0 No.76025 in charge, standing in Ringwood station on 11th April 1964. The track in the foreground was formerly used by trains on the Christchurch line, which dated from 1862. This was at one time part of the principal route from London to Bournemouth and the covered bay platform indicates its former important role. It lost this status when the direct line via Sway opened and was immediately reduced to a purely local line, surviving until September 1935. Passenger services between Brockenhurst and Wimborne ceased from 4th May 1964. *RP*

The 19-mile long Salisbury to Wimborne (West Moors) line, which was promoted by the Salisbury & Dorset Junction Railway, opened for traffic on 20th December 1866. It was absorbed by the LSWR in 1883. The route traversed a very sparsely populated area and the train service reflected this, there rarely being more than seven trains each way on weekdays even during the line's most prosperous times. On summer Saturdays in the 1950s it was sometimes used by through holiday trains between Bournemouth and South Wales. In this illustration BR Standard Class 4MT 2-6-0 No.76067 enters Downton with the 10.30am Bournemouth West to Salisbury train on 14th October 1961. This is famous as the location of a serious incident in 1884 when a train was derailed due to high speed and decayed track. Numerous loose chairs were apparently noticed by the local rector's daughter, who was obviously an extremely vigilant lady. *RP*

The next station down the line was Breamore which was provided with a fully signalled passing loop, but only one siding. The loop line, which is nearest to the camera, was extended just after the Second World War to accommodate longer trains. There used to be a signal box here, located adjacent to where the photographer was standing, but in an effort to reduce costs it was replaced by a lever frame on the up platform in July 1930, thus enabling the station to be operated by one man. Like other stations on this line, Breamore's buildings were woefully neglected by BR, almost as if the managers at Waterloo had forgotten they existed at all! But at least the premises had the luxury of electric lighting. An April 1964 picture. *JP*

A portrait of Fordingbridge station taken on 14th October 1961, looking in the direction of Salisbury. Fordingbridge had the highest population of any intermediate settlement on the Salisbury to Wimborne line and consequently the station's main buildings and goods shed were the largest on the route. There was a passing loop controlled by a 12-lever signal box and, at least in the early days, locomotives heading towards Salisbury were able to take water from a tank adjacent to the bridge. *RP*

Even the usually sleepy country station of Fordingbridge had its moments and in this busy scene (at least by the standards of the Salisbury to Wimborne line!) Maunsell U Class 2-6-0 No.31801 approaches the station at the head of a Bournemouth West to Salisbury service as BR Standard Class 4MT 2-6-0 No.76056 waits in the loop platform with a westbound train. This photograph was taken on 7th July 1962. *CG*

The tiny station of Daggons Road opened for business as 'Daggens Road' in 1876, unlike the others which opened with the line, and consequently the station buildings are in a different style which probably accounts for the lack of a platform canopy. Note that, despite the very modest size of the station, there is a variety of platform furniture, including two different styles of seats and barrows plus some rather ornate oil lamps. There was a brickworks just north of the station that used to be served by a siding and at one time this produced pottery which was sent by rail. Like other stations on this line, years of neglect by BR had taken their toll and by the time of this picture, October 1961, most of the paintwork was in such poor condition that large areas of bare wood were visible where the surface was exposed to the prevailing wind and rain. *RP*

Photographed on 12th October 1963, M7 Class 0-4-4T No.30108 waits to leave Wareham with the 11.10am departure to Swanage. The push-pull train is standing in the down bay platform with the locomotive on the rear, hence the tail lamp on the front of the engine. Hopefully, one day, passengers will once again be able to 'change at Wareham for Swanage'. *LD*

Many of Swanage's residents were hostile to the idea of a railway coming to the town and were determined to fight any such proposal, so schemes put forward in 1847, 1862 and 1877 were all abandoned following fierce opposition from local people. One of the most prominent supporters of the last-mentioned scheme was Mr. George Burt of Swanage who pledged to fight on and he eventually managed to convince the doubters that a connection with the main line at Wareham would be to the town's advantage. In 1880 a bill was deposited in Parliament and in July of the following year an Act authorising construction of the Swanage branch received the Royal Assent. The line opened for passenger traffic on 27th May 1885. It was run by a local company for the first year, but the LSWR soon took over and later bought the branch outright. The line traverses the Isle of Purbeck that has an immense charm and character all of its own, one of its best-known landmarks being Corfe Castle, the ramparts of which also provide an absolutely magnificent bird's-eye view of Corfe Castle station and the surrounding landscape. Even when the weather conditions are unfavourable the vista is breathtaking, as seen here in this illustration of the 1.23pm Swanage to Waterloo heading towards Wareham on 12th August 1961 with an unidentified Bulleid Pacific in charge. The local Hants & Dorset bus seems to have timed its appearance perfectly! *GD*

Looking out from Corfe Castle in a southerly direction the Waterloo train featured in the previous picture can be seen leaving the station, whilst the locomotive of a three-coach push-pull local train bound for Swanage 'blows off' in the down platform. A pair of Pullman camping coaches can just be discerned in the goods yard. As a result of the tireless efforts of members of the Swanage Railway, who rebuilt the railway virtually from scratch, similar photographs can still be taken today, but it is unlikely that the main road winding through the streets of Corfe will be as un-congested as it was when this shot was taken! *GD*

The frontage of Corfe Castle station is depicted in this photograph which was taken from the station approach road on 12th August 1961. Solidly-built of local Purbeck stone, with a roof of red tiles, the station consisted of the usual facilities for passengers, but also incorporated a sizeable house for the use of the station master. This included a scullery on the platform side with a living room and kitchen on the road side. There were four large bedrooms upstairs, so the premises were obviously quite commodious. Few major alterations were made to the station buildings over the years, except for the loss of the down platform's tall LSWR wooden signal box in 1956 which was demolished and replaced by a ground frame on the opposite platform. *GD*

A Swanage to Wareham push-pull train, propelled by M7 Class 0-4-4T No.30667, pauses at Corfe Castle station on a sunny 24th August 1963. These locomotives had been associated with the Swanage branch for around 30 years, but by the time of this picture the remaining examples were reported to be thoroughly worn out which was apparently reflected in their poor performance. The year 1963 proved to be their last full year of operation on the Swanage branch and the remaining representatives of this long-lived class were withdrawn in June 1964, being ousted by BR Standard and Ivatt 2-6-2T locomotives. This change no doubt met with the approval of the engine crews! No.30667 was sent to Eastleigh Works for cutting-up, but at about that time BR policy was changed and it was ordained that condemned locomotives would henceforth be sold to private scrap dealers, and No.30667 was despatched to Briton Ferry, in South Wales, during September 1964. *GH*

A general view of Swanage station taken on 30th July 1961 at the height of the summer holiday period, as evidenced here by the rakes of carriages in (what was supposed to be!) the goods yard. Note also the delightful line of vintage motor coaches, the one nearest to the camera apparently being a Southdown vehicle. The BR parcels delivery van in carmine and cream livery was no doubt kept particularly busy at this time of year distributing holiday-makers' luggage around the town. The M7 Class locomotive simmering in the middle of the picture is No.30057. The principal buildings seen in this photograph were constructed in the local Purbeck stone. Swanage station underwent some structural alterations in the 1930s to cope with the increasing number of visitors, the booking hall and waiting rooms being almost doubled in size. The platform canopy dates from this period. The line's sad decline during the 1960s was reflected in the closure of the goods yard, which ceased operation in October 1965, whilst the signal box was closed in June 1967. Following closure of the line by BR in January 1972 some of the land on the right was sold for development, a supermarket subsequently being built on the site. *RP*

Most railway lovers have their favourite line, but the Somerset & Dorset (S&D) somehow seemed to be everybody's favourite. Unbeatable scenery, beautifully maintained stations, unusual combinations of locomotives and formidable gradients, the S&D was an absolutely wonderful line if ever there was one! The S&D was created as a result of the amalgamation of the Dorset Central Railway and Somerset Central Railway which met near Cole, north of Wincanton, in 1862. The S&D's main line originally ran from Wimborne to Burnham-on-Sea, but when the Bath Extension opened in 1874 through running between Bath and Bournemouth became possible and the status of the line to Burnham was diminished. A spur line between Broadstone and Corfe Mullen opened in 1885, eliminating time-consuming reversals at Wimborne. In this photograph the 4.41pm Bailey Gate to Templecombe train, headed by BR Standard Class 3MT No.82001, awaits departure from Bailey Gate station on 31st March 1962. This train was booked to convey milk tanks as required, but presumably none were available on this day. This class of locomotive is not especially associated with the S&D line, but by the date of this picture the Western Region had gained control of the northern half of the line and two members of this Swindon-built class, Nos.82001 and 82002, had been allocated to Templecombe. *RP*

BOURNEMOUTH TO BATH (GREEN PARK)

The S&D line, as previously mentioned, was famous for its lovingly maintained stations, some of which regularly won prizes in the regional 'Best Kept Station' competitions that took place annually. When this picture was taken at Shillingstone, on 29th October 1965, the closure of the S&D line had already been announced and many of the stations were looking neglected and untidy, as seen here, where the weeds are starting to gain a hold. The train, powered by an equally neglected BR Standard Class 4MT 2-6-0 No.76011, hauling a BR Standard 3-set of coaches, was heading for Bournemouth. *RJ*

Another scene at Shillingstone, taken on 31st March 1962, this time showing former GWR 2251 Class 0-6-0 No.2219 leaving in charge of a Poole to Templecombe freight train. The Western Region's takeover of part of the S&D route was manifested in the increasing use of these engines; in the late 1950s this particular example was based at Oswestry for use on the Cambrian lines. Shillingstone's 16-lever signal box is visible on the right. The small goods yard, which is partly visible, also on the right of the shot, was closed on 5th April 1965. *RP*

The 3.23pm train to Templecombe waits to leave Evercreech Junction station on 20th July 1963. 2251 Class 0-6-0 No.2204 is in charge and the train is formed of a GWR-designed brake second, immediately behind the locomotive, and a BR Standard non-corridor second-class vehicle. BR Standard Class 5MT No.73052 is taking water on the left. Evercreech Junction was an important intermediate station on the S&D line where the branch line to Highbridge (regular services to Burnham-on-Sea ceased in 1951) diverged from the main line to Bath. There was a large goods yard north of the station, just discernible in the distance, and a turntable which was mainly used to turn locomotives arriving on freight workings. In the days when the S&D route carried substantial summer Saturday holiday traffic the middle siding was used to stable locomotives waiting to pilot heavy northbound expresses over the Mendip Hills to Bath. Unsuspecting passengers must have been amazed to find as many as five steam engines, usually LMSR 2P Class 4-4-0s, awaiting their turn to assist northbound trains. *GH*

The S&D line, as previously mentioned, passed through some beautiful countryside, one of the loveliest sections being between Midford and Bath. Here the 2.00pm Templecombe to Bath (Green Park) train, with an unidentified BR Standard Class 4MT 2-6-4T in charge, is seen crossing Tucking Mill viaduct, in Horsecombe Vale, on 4th March 1966. The train is climbing up to Combe Down tunnel, on a single-line section that was a notorious bottleneck on busy summer Saturdays. If the railway authorities had had their way the S&D route would have been closed to passenger trains from 3rd January 1966, but one of the road operators who was to have provided alternative bus services withdrew his application for a licence at the last minute and the closure was deferred for two months. An emergency service was introduced, the train depicted here being one of only four advertised passenger workings from Templecombe to Bath. The following two days saw a final flurry of rail tours before the S&D line was finally laid to rest – a sad end to an outstanding route. *GH*

The S&D line had a long tradition of individuality which was one of its hallmarks. This is exemplified by this photograph, taken on 16th July 1960, at Glastonbury & Street station, on the Highbridge branch, which shows the remarkable combination of a Southern Railway notice in the foreground with an unidentified veteran Midland Railway Class 3F 0-6-0 shunting in the background. The view is looking west from the station. For many years this line was the domain of these Johnson-designed Class 3F locomotives and their 0-4-4T cousins, and representatives of both classes were based at Highbridge shed for working the branch. JL

Glastonbury & Street station is also the location of this picture, taken on the same day as the previous shot, which shows Ivatt Class 2MT 2-6-2T No.41248 pausing with the 9.45am Highbridge to Templecombe train. The train in the other platform is the 9.55am from Evercreech Junction to Highbridge. The outer face of the platform on the right used to be used by trains to Wells (Priory Road) but these were an early casualty, closure taking place from 29th October 1951. Clarks shoes at one time despatched boxes of their well-known commodity by rail, whilst the local sawmill, which had its own siding, also provided traffic for the railway. JL

A scene at Edington Burtle station on 20th July 1963 with Ivatt 2-6-2T No.41242 in charge of a train to Highbridge. The premises here were clearly overdue for painting: note the wartime stripes on the canopy stanchions! This station opened as Edington Road in 1856 and became Edington Junction when the line to Bridgwater was opened in July 1890. Trains to Bridgwater, which used the bay platform on the right, were discontinued from 1st December 1952 and this resulted in the station's name being changed to Edington Burtle. In 1956 the signal box was closed and 1964 saw the withdrawal of goods facilities. *GH*

EVERCREECH JUNCTION TO HIGHBRIDGE

The main line from Waterloo to Exeter was inconveniently sited for passengers travelling to Yeovil, taking a course almost two miles south of the town, so a short branch was opened from Yeovil Junction, on the main line, to Yeovil Town station which was situated in the town centre. The link was opened by the LSWR on 1st June 1861. A shuttle service was operated between the two stations and this was formed of a LSWR M7 Class 0-4-4T with a push-pull set for many years, before it was 'Westernised' with a pannier tank and auto coach. Here No.30129 'blows off' impatiently in the evening sunshine prior to leaving Yeovil Junction with the 6.33pm to the Town station on 18th August 1962.
The main line tracks veer off to the right in the background. *JP*

A breathtaking panoramic view of Yeovil Town station and its environs: this scene was recorded on 26th March 1964. Apart from the Bulleid Pacific resting 'on shed', the locomotives seem to be entirely BR Standard types. The road vehicles are worthy of attention, especially the Royal Blue long-distance coach, which was probably *en route* from London to Exeter. The double-decker vehicles were operated by Southern National which ran local services in the area, but the identity of the coach waiting in the goods yard is a mystery; maybe it was a military vehicle. Yeovil's first train service was provided by the Bristol & Exeter Railway which obtained an Act of Parliament in 1845 to construct a broad gauge line from Durston Junction, on the Taunton to Bristol line, to Hendford on the western fringe of Yeovil. It should be noted that the Taunton to Westbury line did not open until many years later. Hendford station opened on 1st October 1853. The next major development in the area was the opening throughout of the Frome to Weymouth line on 20th January 1857. The main line from Sherborne was brought into regular use on 1st June 1860, trains using a spur line from Bradford Abbas which took them across the Weymouth route and into Hendford station where they connected with those on the broad gauge. At least one train in each direction on the main line to Exeter (which was brought into use on 19th July 1860) ran to and from Hendford. Powers to build Yeovil Town station, where both the Bristol & Exeter and 'South Western' trains could be better accommodated, were granted on 14th June 1860 and the new station opened on 1st June 1861. From that date Hendford was reduced in status to a goods yard. The line from Yeovil Town to Taunton closed in June 1964, whilst trains continued to run between the Town and Junction stations until 3rd October 1966. *GD*

In the 1840s there were some incredibly ambitious schemes for routes linking the Bristol and English channels, one being for a Watchet to Bridport line! Most of these were planned to pass near to Chard, but the first line to serve Chard was actually the 3¼-mile long branch from Chard Road (later Chard Junction), on the LSWR Yeovil to Exeter line, to Chard Town station, which opened on 8th May 1863. Not quite as exciting as the Watchet to Bridport route, perhaps, but at least it did become a reality! On 11th September 1866 the Bristol & Exeter Railway's (B&ER) broad gauge line from Taunton arrived on the scene in Chard, the station being named 'Chard Joint' and this new station catered for both companies, Chard Town later being closed. The GWR, successors to the B&ER, took over operation of the entire line from 1st January 1917. Chard Joint station was renamed Chard Central by BR in 1949 and during the following year the SR took control of the complete branch, only for it to revert to WR administration in 1958. Passenger trains were withdrawn from 10th September 1962 after many years of decline. This picture shows pannier tank locomotive No.7436 waiting at Chard Junction with the 5.50pm train to Chard Central on 24th June 1961. Note that trains on this line used a platform that was separated from the main line station by a roadway. The picture is deceptive because the plume of steam is being emitted from an engine standing in the main station, not the pannier tank locomotive! *JL*

CHARD JUNCTION TO CHARD TOWN

The Seaton branch was promoted by the Seaton & Beer Railway which obtained its Act on 13th July 1863 and the line opened to passengers, apparently without ceremony, on 16th March 1868. The 4¼-mile long line, which was worked by the LSWR from the outset, ran from Seaton Junction station, on the main London to Exeter route, and passed through Colyton and Colyford before arriving at Seaton. The station, which was built on the west bank of the River Axe, was very conveniently situated being practically on the seafront. Traffic on the branch was mainly seasonal, however, and this proved to be its undoing, the line being tabled for closure in the Beeching Report. The branch was closed completely from 7th March 1966. During its twilight years the line was worked by diesel units, but about a year before closure there was a shortage of units during which time steam traction made a temporary comeback. By this time the branch was firmly under Western Region control and consequently 1400 Class 0-4-2Ts and auto trailers were brought in to fill the breach, a quite extraordinary development. In this shot No.1450 stands at Seaton Junction station on 13th February 1965 before setting off down the branch. *RD*

The small intermediate station of Colyton is depicted in this shot which was taken on 6th April 1963. A small goods yard with two sidings and a brick-built shed were originally provided here, and there was a tiny signal box which lasted until 1922 but was used as a ground frame until 1958. Goods facilities were withdrawn from 3rd February 1964. In August 1970 the 2ft 9in gauge Seaton & District Tramway, which employed equipment previously used at Eastbourne, opened between Seaton and Colyford as a tourist attraction. In 1980 the line was extended to Colyton, so it is still possible to travel over much of the old branch line. *GH*

The picturesque 6¾-mile long Axminster to Lyme Regis branch is probably one of the best-remembered branches featured in this book. It was very much a latecomer on the scene, being opened as a light railway on 24th August 1903. The route had some very steep gradients in addition to notoriously tight curves and these characteristics restricted the type of motive power that could be used. At first, LBSCR 'Terriers', which had been especially purchased by the LSWR, were employed but they were soon superseded by Class O2 0-4-4Ts. The first-mentioned tended to spread the track whilst the latter suffered from excessive flange wear due to the extremely tight curves. In 1913 the Adams 'Radial' 4-4-2Ts took over the workings and proved an immediate success, so beginning an association with the line that lasted until 1961. In this portrait Adams 'Radial' No.30583 eases out of the bay platform at Axminster with a two-coach train to Lyme Regis on 18th June 1960 while a main line train waits in the up main platform. The line climbed away from the station at 1 in 80 before crossing the main line on a bridge. At one time there was a connection on the down side but this ceased operation in about 1915. *RD*

The 4.36pm Axminster to Lyme Regis train is seen shortly after leaving Axminster on 4th June 1960, with No.30583 striding along sedately with a typical two-coach formation. This was the last full year of the Adams 'Radial' locomotives' operation on the branch. The coaches are both Maunsell-designed vehicles, a brake composite corridor immediately behind the locomotive, whilst the rear coach is a second open carriage. *JT*

Combpyne was the sole intermediate station on the branch and in this shot No.30584 is depicted hauling the 2.28pm train from Axminster on 19th June 1960. Judging by the row of sleepers, the permanent way people had presumably been relaying the track and easing the curves to accommodate larger locomotives. The station purported to serve a small settlement of the same name but villagers wishing to use the train were confronted with a ¾-mile uphill walk to the station, which no doubt deterred all but the most determined travellers. There was a little bit of goods traffic at Combpyne, but this was confined to the occasional consignment of fertilizer or agricultural produce. *RP*

An attempt was made in November 1958 to replace the Adams tank locomotives but the trials of a GWR 1400 0-4-2T were unsuccessful. Ivatt Class 2MT 2-6-2Ts were eventually introduced on a regular basis in early 1961 following track alterations and in this picture No.41307 is seen pausing at Combpyne on 13th February 1965. By this date the line had been worked by diesel units for some time but steam traction had temporarily re-appeared due to a shortage of units. The one-coach train is comprised of a BR Standard brake composite vehicle (BCK) which, as its name implies, offered both first and second-class accommodation. Until 1930 Combpyne was a crossing station, but during that year the loop connection was removed at one end and signalling dismantled: the siding created was used to stable a camping coach. The redundant signal box found further use locally as a farm outbuilding. The milk churns in the foreground were used to convey domestic water from Lyme Regis. On a warm summer's evening Combpyne station must have been a really peaceful, idyllic spot where the sound of birdsong was only occasionally disturbed by passing trains. *RD*

Viewed from a quiet country lane down in the valley, Adams 'Radial' tank locomotive No.30583 takes the 10.00am Lyme Regis to Axminster train across Cannington viaduct on 4th June 1960. This machine probably had the most eventful life of any locomotive illustrated in this album. It was built as LSWR No.488 in 1885 by Neilson & Co. Ltd of Glasgow for use on suburban services from Waterloo. In 1917 it was sold out of service to the Ministry of Munitions who put it to work at the Ridham salvage depot, Sittingbourne, but it did not last long there, being sold again two years later to the East Kent Railway (EKR) where it remained for many years, becoming No.5 in their series. Two other Adams 'Radial' locomotives were used on the Lyme Regis branch, but by 1946 both were in need of extensive repairs and the Southern Railway approached the EKR regarding No.5 which by this time was lying out of use at Shepherdswell. The EKR readily agreed to sell No.5 and the locomotive was moved to Eastleigh where it received a thorough overhaul, prior to taking up its duties on the Lyme Regis branch. *JT*

The only engineering work of any consequence on the Lyme Regis branch was Cannington viaduct which was one of the earliest examples built by 'Concrete Bob' McAlpine. The 10-arch structure is 203 yards long and 93ft high. Trains from Axminster approached the viaduct on a 1 in 40 falling gradient but this eased to 1 in 82 across the viaduct. The 10.37am from Axminster coasts down the incline, also on 4th June 1960, the day the previous shot was taken. The viaduct has always been marred by its drooped appearance at one end, this being a legacy of subsidence that occurred during construction. A jack arch had to be constructed in the third span to prevent further settlement, thus rather spoiling the symmetry of the structure. *JT*

The elegant lines of Adams 'Radial' No.30583 are clearly seen in this portrait of the locomotive hauling the 12.38pm Axminster to Lyme Regis train on 18th June 1960. This is a panned shot, hence the train is sharp, but the rest of the picture is blurred. The Settle to Carlisle, West Highland and Cambrian Coast lines are generally regarded as being classic routes, but surely the Lyme Regis branch's tortuous curves, formidable gradients, unique motive power and beautiful scenery qualified it for a similar description? *GD*

Shortly before arriving in Lyme Regis trains crossed the county boundary into Dorset and quick-sighted passengers could obtain a glimpse of the sea before their train entered the station. The station there was rather inconveniently sited 250ft above sea level and yet the sea was only half a mile distant: it is only too evident why the line could not penetrate nearer to the town. The premises had only one platform face with a run-round loop and in this portrait, taken on 18th June 1960, No.30583 is apparently setting back into the platform after running round. Lyme Regis had a 14-lever wooden signal box, which is prominent in the picture, and a small engine shed, part of which is just visible to the right of the engine. The latter closed on 4th November 1963 when steam operation officially ended on the branch. There were also three sidings, one of which served a small goods shed. *RD*

The route between Crediton and Barnstaple was promoted by the North Devon Railway and came into use on 1st August 1854 as a continuation of the broad gauge Exeter & Crediton Railway which had been opened on 12th May 1851. There had been acrimonious disputes about the gauge between the Bristol & Exeter Railway and LSWR as the latter saw Crediton as an ideal base from where to start its drive into the far west. The 'South Western' company apparently engaged in some underhand share dealings through which it gained control of the Exeter & Crediton Company from 1st February 1862 and immediately laid a third running rail to enable standard gauge trains to operate. An extra rail was also installed throughout to Barnstaple and dual gauge operations commenced on this section from 2nd March 1863. Broad gauge trains continued to work to Barnstaple until 30th April 1877 and to Crediton, which was the last surviving broad gauge outpost in the area, until 1892. After leaving Crediton, Copplestone (seen here) was the first station on the North Devon line and, indeed, is also the highest point on the route, standing at 350ft above sea level. Copplestone also marked the end of the brief double-track section of line from Coleford Junction, where the Okehampton line diverged, and the end of the double track from Waterloo. The station building was a substantial stone-built structure and included a station house besides the usual passenger facilities. The 10-lever signal box, on the right, dated from 1873 and lasted until 17th October 1971 when the line was singled southwards. The goods yard was closed from 6th October 1965. This picture was taken on 18th May 1964. *DS*

On this and the next page are three views taken at Portsmouth Arms station on 18th May 1964 which perfectly portray the idyllic setting of this small, but beautifully maintained, rural station. The station's main entrance, with its neat display of posters, is seen in this picture. One of the posters appears to be a closure notice, perhaps for the Barnstaple Junction to Torrington line which lost its passenger trains eighteen months after this shot was taken. Another, rather inappropriate, poster is advertising the service that BR provided to heavy industry, not that there was very much around Portsmouth Arms station nor, indeed, in the whole of Devon! *DS*

Portsmouth Arms station nestles amid rolling hills that form the backdrop to this portrait of the delightful station building which was located on the down platform. There is no settlement of any size nearby, the station being literally 'in the middle of nowhere' in true British branch line tradition! The station's name was taken from the nearby public house which in turn was named after the Earl of Portsmouth who was, apparently, one of the financiers of the adjacent turnpike road. There was a reasonably long loop at Portsmouth Arms which could accommodate eight-coach trains: only occasional peak holiday trains would have exceeded this length. *DS*

The Portsmouth Arms signalman's daily routine was only occasionally disturbed by passing trains and in this picture an unidentified un-rebuilt Bulleid Pacific is seen 'blowing off' impatiently prior to leaving with a northbound working. The signal box dated from 1873 and it was taken out of use, together with the up loop, in April 1966. The scooter no doubt belonged to the signalman, whose drinking water was delivered every day in a large can. Note the milepost which indicates the distance from Waterloo: 200½ miles. What an absorbing spot this must have been in steam days, especially on a summer Saturday in the 1950s when holiday traffic was at its height before the growth of private car ownership and cheap continental holidays destroyed this traffic forever. *DS*

A study of M7 Class 0-4-4T No.30254, which is in quite clean condition, pausing between shunting duties at Barnstaple Junction station on 5th August 1961. This machine was built at the LSWR's Nine Elms works in August 1897 and survived to become one of the very last members of the class in traffic, being withdrawn in May 1964. *RD*

No fewer than four steam locomotives are visible, or at least partially visible, in this picture of Barnstaple Junction station which was also taken on 5th August 1961. The tracks on the left led to Barnstaple Town station, just across the river Taw, and Ilfracombe. The main station building, which was designed by Sir William Tite, is on the left, whilst Barnstaple 'B' signal box is just out of the shot in bottom left hand corner. The large roofs, visible above the covered footbridge, are those of the goods depot and locomotive shed. The very distinctive track layout, with its many check rails, is a reminder of the days before the standardisation of permanent way components. Note especially the sharply curved three-way point on the left of the picture over which the M7 Class engine is passing. Today the station is a pale shadow of what it was at the time of this photograph and only a single platform survives. All of the trackwork beyond the platform end has completely gone and even the footbridge, which no longer served any purpose, has disappeared. How terribly sad! *RD*

The 15 miles-long Barnstaple to Ilfracombe line is well known for its extremely steep gradients which made the line a difficult one to operate, especially during the summer months when heavy holiday trains ran. Down trains faced a 1 in 40 incline up to Mortehoe & Woolacombe station which was located 600ft above sea level, a climb that was made even more difficult by the tortuous nature of the route as it swung wildly through the Caen Valley. In the opposite direction there was a 1 in 36 climb away from Ilfracombe station which commenced immediately at the platform end and continued until just before Mortehoe station was reached. So working a heavily-laden train over this demanding section of railway was not a task for faint-hearted enginemen, even when an assisting engine was provided! The line was proposed by a subsidiary of the LSWR which received Royal Assent on 4th July 1870. Construction was delayed by the need to undertake substantial earthworks and the line's opening did not take place until 20th July 1874. Another factor in this delay was the necessity to build a bridge across the River Taw, seen here in this picture taken from the 2.55pm Ilfracombe to Waterloo train on 12th September 1959. Motive power is provided by Bulleid Pacific No.34023 *Blackmore Vale* whilst the leading Bulleid 3-set of coaches is Set 981, one of only four sets of this type which were comprised entirely of compartment vehicles built on long underframes. Note also the bogie van (known as a 'Van B') halfway down the train. How absolutely fascinating railways used to be! *JL*

For any steam enthusiast one of the most exhilarating experiences was to lean out of a train window to listen to the sound of the exhaust noise being produced by the locomotive. Safety notices always warned people 'Do not lean out of the window' but the wonderful and exciting feeling of air rushing past one's face as the train sped along at top speed with its engine being worked to the limit often proved irresistible to many foolhardy enthusiasts, including the author! Sometimes, of course, smuts from the engine would finish up in one's eye, but that discomfort was a small price to pay if one wanted to experience the thrill of raw steam power! It is unlikely that the train was speeding along when this picture was taken but, even so, the memories of many readers will be rekindled by this shot from the leading coach of the 8.54am Waterloo to Ilfracombe on 12th September 1959 as it nears Wrafton, north of Barnstaple, behind an unkempt Bulleid 'Battle of Britain' Pacific No.34079 *141 Squadron*. The 8.54am which was, in effect, a relief to the 9.00am, left London formed of thirteen coaches, but only five remained by the time this picture was taken. The other train is the 2.20pm from Ilfracombe, in charge of an unidentified Maunsell N Class 2-6-0. *JL*

BARNSTAPLE TO ILFRACOMBE

The owner of Lake's Private Hotel at Braunton no doubt mentioned its close proximity to Saunton Sands and Croyde Bay to intending guests, but one wonders if he referred to the hotel's perfect situation for visiting train spotters! Patrons staying in the front bedrooms could almost look straight down the chimney of passing locomotives. What a superb attraction, but probably one that did not get even the briefest mention in the establishment's brochure! In this portrait M7 Class 0-4-4T No.30251 simmers in the down platform on 12th September 1959. Braunton was at the foot of the severe climb, mostly at 1 in 40 or thereabouts, to Mortehoe, so perhaps the M7 was waiting to assist a down train. Even quite lightly loaded trains had to be helped up the bank and it must have been a thrilling sight and sound as the two locomotives heaved their train up to the summit at Mortehoe. *JL*

Mortehoe & Woolacombe station was, as previously mentioned, located on the 600ft contour and the summit of tremendous climbs in both directions. In times past enginemen working heavy trains must have been relieved when the station came into view. The signalman no doubt had a particularly busy time on summer Saturdays when banking engines needed to use the crossover to return 'home' after assisting a train from either Braunton or Ilfracombe. The station was about two miles from both the village of Mortehoe and the small resort of Woolacombe. This must have been a bleak and windswept spot in the winter when gales swept in off the Atlantic, hence the main station buildings (on the down side) were rendered with cement as added protection against the weather. This shot was taken on 24th August 1963. *DS*

The line from Barnstaple to Torrington has a complex history and the section as far as Bideford has, at various times, been operated as a broad, dual and then standard gauge line. The first railway between Barnstaple and Fremington was a standard gauge horse-worked line built with the intention of conveying cargo from a planned new dock at Fremington to Barnstaple. It was proposed by the Taw Vale Railway & Dock Company which obtained its Act on 11th June 1838 and the line opened on 25th April 1848. The line was later converted to broad gauge and passenger services commenced running to Fremington on 1st August 1854. An extension to Bideford, also broad gauge, was opened on 2nd November 1855. In 1862 the LSWR appeared on the scene, taking over the lease of the Taw Vale Company and converting the Bideford line to dual gauge, with the result that standard gauge trains started running to Bideford from 2nd March 1863. Goods trains continued to use the broad gauge track until April 1877. The LSWR proposed a further extension, this time from Bideford to Torrington, and it obtained an Act for its construction on 19th June 1865: the line opened on 18th July 1872. The River Taw is visible in the background of this picture which shows an unidentified Ivatt Class 2MT 2-6-2T (thought to be No.41314) approaching Barnstaple Junction with a two-coach local train from Torrington on 24th April 1960. *RD*

A train for Torrington drifts in to Fremington on 24th August 1963 behind Ivatt Class 2MT 2-6-2T No.41283. The rather distinctive signal box dominates the picture and looks as though it was designed to give signalmen a good view out to sea as well as railway operations! The box lasted until 3rd November 1968, when it was taken out of commission. The principal commodity imported at Fremington was coal and much of it was for railway use at motive power depots in the Exeter area. Other traffic included china clay, which was shipped to various European destinations, and timber. The quay was closed on 31st December 1969. *DS*

Taken from the four-coach Torrington portion of the down 'Atlantic Coast Express' hauled by M7 0-4-4T No.30255, this shot shows the layout of the sidings alongside the quay at Fremington. Note the steam cranes and spilt china clay on the ground. The small port of Fremington was modernised by the Southern Railway in the 1930s and reputedly became the busiest port in Devon, apart from Plymouth. This picture was taken on 12th September 1959. *JL*

Today's modern train operating companies appear to be very concerned about their 'image' and signs on stations are an important part of this obsession. In past times British Railways were, one might say, a little more relaxed about such things, as exemplified here by this picture taken at Torrington which shows a Southern Railway sign still proudly displayed many years after nationalisation. The train standing in the platform is the 4.40pm to Halwill Junction, with Ivatt Class 2MT No.41295 in charge, and this picture was also taken on 12th September 1959. *JL*

In 1914 the North Devon & Cornwall Junction Light Railway obtained an order under the Light Railways Act to construct a standard gauge line from Torrington to Halwill. The first 6½ miles were to be built on the course of the 3ft gauge mineral line between Torrington and Marland that had been built in 1880 for the transportation of china clay. Delayed by the outbreak of the First World War, construction eventually began in 1922 with the legendary light-railway builder Col. H.F. Stephens as engineer. It proved to be the last such line built under his direction. The line was a classic railway backwater and passed through very sparsely populated countryside, its main purpose being to serve china clay workings in the area, especially at Marland and Meeth. The route opened on 27th July 1925 and was operated from the outset by the Southern Railway. A journey on the line no doubt provided one of the most restful and enjoyable branch line rambles one could wish for, and certainly one that was unlikely to be disturbed by other passengers! In this portrait the train depicted in the previous illustration is seen at Hatherleigh which was the only intermediate settlement of any size on the branch. During his journey the photographer noted only three other passengers, one of whom was a member of BR staff! *JL*

Another picture of the Torrington to Halwill Junction line taken on 12th September 1959: this view shows the station of Hole for Black Torrington. The name Hole (which was used to avoid confusion with Torrington) apparently refers to a small group of nearby houses whilst Black Torrington is a hamlet a mile or so distant. Note the goods wagons in the yard: freight facilities survived here until September 1964. *JL*

This fine specimen of an LSWR running-in board, painted incongruously in Western Region brown, was photographed at Halwill Junction, also on 12th September 1959. This remote country junction was where the lines to Bude and Torrington diverged from the Okehampton to Wadebridge route. All of these routes were extremely attractive, but they traversed very thinly populated areas and were hopelessly uneconomic. Trains ran from Halwill to Torrington until October 1965, whilst those on the remaining routes lasted exactly a year longer. The network of closed SR lines west of Exeter, which became known as the 'Withered Arm', had an immense character all of its own and its loss is still mourned by many railway aficionados. *JL*

Train services between Exeter and Okehampton commenced on 3rd October 1871. In 1873 the Devon & Cornwall Railway obtained an Act to construct a line westwards from Okehampton to Holsworthy which was intended to branch off from the (then incomplete) Okehampton to Lydford route at Meldon Junction. The line to Holsworthy opened to passengers on 20th January 1879. The next development was in August 1882 when the North Cornwall Railway, which was promoted by the LSWR, obtained an Act to build a line from Halwill Junction (on the Holsworthy route) to Launceston and Padstow. Progress was slowed by the shortage of funds plus the difficult terrain and it was 21st July 1886 before the first section opened as far as Launceston. Wadebridge was eventually reached, services commencing on 1st June 1895, whilst it was almost another four years before the short section along the river Camel estuary to Padstow was completed. This final stretch opened on 27th March 1899. It is debatable whether this picture qualifies for inclusion in an album about branch lines, because the train seen here was hardly a branch service. It is, however, quite an intriguing photograph because it depicts an especially interesting and short-lived service that was rarely photographed in colour, the Surbiton to Okehampton car-carrier train that only operated during the summer season between 1960 and 1964. The working depicted is the 8.03am Surbiton-Okehampton on arrival at its destination on 21st July 1962: the passenger and car-carrying sections of the train had already been separated when this shot was taken. Strangely, all but one of the General Utility Vans used to convey the cars appear to have been recently repainted whilst, remarkably, one of the three passenger-carrying coaches is a Maunsell-designed 'nondescript' brake vehicle, a type not usually seen so far west. The platforms seen here dated back to at least the First World War and were formerly used for military traffic to and from the training areas on Dartmoor. The photographer was on a cycling tour at the time and perhaps later headed off into the fabulous countryside which forms such a memorable and stunning backdrop to this fascinating scene. *JT*

A down train bound for Padstow passes Meldon Quarry, which is out of sight behind the train, behind a rather unkempt Bulleid 'Battle of Britain' Class Pacific No.34070 *Manston* on 27th June 1964. The building on the right of the picture is the compressor house. The train is quite a long one for the North Cornwall line and its six-coach length suggests that it may have been the 'Atlantic Coast Express'. *GH*

Photographed at an absolutely unmistakable location, an unidentified train bound for the North Cornwall line crosses Meldon viaduct on 27th June 1964: motive power is provided by Maunsell N Class 'Mogul' No.31854. The spindly-looking viaduct, which is 199 miles from Waterloo, consists of six 86½ft spans built on stone plinths and the structure rises to a height of 150ft above the valley floor at its highest point. The viaduct was constructed on a 30-chain curve and carries the railway across a deep ravine through which flows the West Okement river, a tributary of the river Torridge. The summit of the route, which was approached from the east on gradients varying between 1 in 58 and 1 in 77, was located about a mile west of here, near Meldon Junction. Part of Meldon Quarry can be seen in the background. *GH*

OKEHAMPTON TO PADSTOW

The vintage LSWR running-in board immediately identifies the location of this picture. The train depicted is a morning mixed working to Wadebridge with N Class 'Mogul' No.31849 in charge and this picture was taken on 2nd May 1959. In addition to workings on the former LSWR route from Okehampton, Launceston was also served by trains on the former GWR route from Plymouth and the two stations were adjacent to each other. It was clearly uneconomic to have two stations serving a small town and the former GWR premises were closed from 30th June 1952, services being diverted to the former LSWR station from that date using a connection that had been installed during the Second World War. There was a small engine shed and turntable serving Launceston's 'Southern' station, but by 1961 the shed was roofless and the building was in a very dilapidated condition. *DS*

Another portrait of Launceston, but this time taken in July 1962, and showing a short, two-coach train heading towards Halwill Junction. The locomotive in charge is BR Standard Class 4MT 2-6-4T No.80064, which subsequently survived into preservation. The former GWR premises were located on the right and continued in use as a goods depot until 1966. Despite the cessation of BR operations here in October 1966, the valley in which Launceston is situated continues to echo to the sound of steam traction because the narrow gauge Launceston Steam Railway was established along part of the trackbed of the old LSWR route in 1983. *DS*

Bulleid 'Battle of Britain' Class Pacific No.34078
222 Squadron rolls into Otterham with the 3.32pm
Okehampton to Padstow train on 25th July 1964.
The summit of the line (800ft above sea level) was
reached just beyond Otterham station. Situated nearly
two miles from the village it purported to serve, the
station was in a bleak, windswept location and some
of the walls of the building were slate-hung to keep
out the worst of the weather. Goods traffic ceased in
September 1964 while the station became unstaffed
from 6th December 1965. *GH*

Another North Cornwall line scene, also recorded on 25th July 1964. The location is Port Isaac Road station and a train bound for Padstow, almost certainly the 10.15am from Okehampton, is seen departing behind BR Standard Class 4MT 2-6-4T No.80039. The tiny goods yard, depicted here in the left foreground, was closed from 7th September 1964. The small coastal village of Port Isaac was located about three miles away, so the station was unlikely to have been busy! *GH*

The area around Kit Hill, just north of Callington, was a centre of mining activity which reached its zenith in the mid-19th century. There was an urgent need to improve transport in an area that was very poorly served and on 7th May 1872 the East Cornwall Mineral Railway (ECMR) opened its 7¾ mile long 3ft 6in gauge line from Kelly Bray, 640 feet above sea level at the foot of Kit Hill, to Calstock Quay. There was a cable-operated incline at Calstock which rose for 35 chains at a gradient of 1 in 6, taking wagons from the quay up to the tramway which was 350 feet higher up the valley. In 1891 the line was taken over by the Plymouth, Devonport & South Western Junction Railway (PDSWJR), which had been incorporated in 1883 to build its route from Lydford to Devonport, this opening in 1890. In 1900 the PDSWJR obtained a Light Railway Order to enable conversion of the ECMR to standard gauge in order to link up with its 'main line' at Bere Alston. This involved the construction of a magnificent 12-arch viaduct with 60ft spans across the river Tamar at Calstock and following its completion the line opened on 2nd March 1908. The incline was replaced by an extremely high wagon lift adjacent to the viaduct and this lasted until about 1934. The LSWR O2 Class locomotives were regular motive power on the branch passenger trains from 1929 until they were displaced by Ivatt 2-6-2Ts. In this picture O2 Class No.30225 steams across the graceful viaduct with a Callington-bound train on 20th May 1961. *GD*

This lifebuoy on Calstock Quay still bore the initials of its original owner when photographed on 29th July 1961. One wonders if it had ever been used! *GH*

Whilst the elderly LSWR O2 Class 0-4-4Ts were not officially replaced by Ivatt 2-6-2Ts on Callington branch passenger services until 1961, the Ivatt-designed locomotives evidently did some work on the passenger services well before this time. In this shot No.41317 pauses at Calstock station with the 11.12am Callington to Bere Alston train on 13th September 1959: this was a Sunday, so perhaps the 2-6-2Ts were sometimes used on Sundays when they would otherwise have been idle. Note the train's remarkable formation, which includes a former LNER van, immediately behind the engine, followed by a former SECR ten-compartment third (designated second class by this date) and a Maunsell-designed BCK. A few seconds after the train left Calstock station it would have been riding 129 feet high above the waters of the river and offering railway passengers exclusive(!), unrivalled views of the Tamar valley. The river forms the county boundary between Devon and Cornwall, only the first 1½ miles of the branch being in Devon before trains crossed the river into Cornwall. *JL*

After leaving Calstock the railway runs in an east-south-easterly direction, often climbing at gradients as steep as 1 in 40, before turning through 180 degrees to run in a roughly north-westerly direction before Gunnislake station is reached. The station there consisted of an island platform, whose striking, perhaps rather gaudy, green and cream regional colours certainly stand out in this shot which was taken on 6th May 1961. Perhaps the premises had recently benefited from work by the SR's station painting team! Judging by the pile on the platform, parcels traffic certainly seemed to be buoyant on the day of the photographer's visit. Gunnislake has been the limit of operations since withdrawal of passenger services beyond there on 7th November 1966. *RP*

PLYMOUTH TO CALLINGTON

When the ECMR opened its line in 1872 the northerly terminus was known as Kelly Bray, the village in which it was located, just over a mile north of Callington. When the route was converted to standard gauge by the PDSWJR the station became Callington Road, until this was abbreviated to just plain Callington in November 1909. The tightly curved approach to the station was typical of the route beyond Calstock. The station and its environs were a delight for any railway enthusiast, the modest terminal being blessed with an overall roof, whilst there was a two-road engine shed for stabling locomotives. Two Ivatt-designed Class 2MT 2-6-2Ts are in the shot taken on 29th July 1961: the locomotive on the left appears to be on shunting duties whilst that on the right was no doubt waiting to leave with a passenger working. *GH*

A closer view of Callington station, also on 29th July 1961, with its overall roof which must have made the interior somewhat gloomy! A rather dirty Ivatt 2-6-2T, No.41302, 'blows off' prior to departure with a train to Bere Alston and Plymouth. Judging by the assortment on the platform Callington clearly possessed a fine collection of platform barrows of varying designs. *GH*

Powers were obtained in 1865 by the Okehampton Railway (later renamed Devon & Cornwall) to build a line to Bude, but these lapsed. A further attempt was made and in 1873 parliamentary approval was given for a line as far as Holsworthy, and opening took place on 20th January 1879. It left the then incomplete route from Okehampton to Lydford at Meldon Junction and meandered 17¾ miles across upland pastures to the town of Holsworthy. The 10½ miles-long extension to Bude was eventually opened by the LSWR on 10th August 1898. In this illustration the original single platform terminal station building is depicted which had a run-round loop prior to the construction of the Bude extension. Holsworthy was a busy centre of the livestock trade that generated much railborne traffic, but all of this was later lost to road competition and when the goods yard closed on 7th September 1964 only fertiliser and coal traffic remained. This picture was taken on 21st July 1962. *JT*

Bude station is depicted in this portrait taken on 13th July 1963. The locomotive in the background on the left of the shot is Maunsell N Class 'Mogul' No.31846. An extremely impressive station building was constructed and included the stationmaster's house with its adjacent garden. The structure boasted a substantial gable and was embellished with stone quoins; there was a dormer window above the booking hall to improve illumination. The principal platform, nearest to the camera, could accommodate up to ten coaches. There was a small locomotive shed at Bude complete with an ash pit and coal dock whilst the local gas works and abattoir were rail connected and doubtless produced much railborne traffic. Perhaps the most interesting aspect of operations at Bude was the half-mile-long line to the canal wharf which remained in use until goods facilities were withdrawn from Bude in September 1964. The branch was dieselised from 2nd January 1965, but the more economical diesel operation failed to save the line and it closed completely from 3rd October 1966. *RP*

At first sight the locomotive depicted in this illustration, Ivatt Class 2MT
No.41272, appears to be carrying a small nameplate beneath the BR totem
on the tankside. Knowledgeable railway aficionados will know, of course,
that none of these engines ever carried an official name and the plate
actually commemorates the fact that No.41272 was the 7,000th locomotive
to be built at Crewe Works, in September 1950. In this picture it is seen at
Wadebridge awaiting departure with a train to Bodmin North in June 1962.
No.41272 was a mere twelve years old when this picture was taken, but the
line over which it was about to work dated from 1834 and was one of the
oldest in Great Britain. The Bodmin & Wadebridge Railway had the
distinction of being the first in Cornwall to be worked by locomotives which
hauled mineral trains, predominantly of sea-sand dredged from the Camel
estuary, but also of china clay and granite for export. The line was acquired
by the LSWR in 1847 but, incredibly, it remained in splendid, physical
isolation from the rest of the system until the LSWR's line from Waterloo
reached Wadebridge in 1895. *DS*

A scene at Bodmin North station on 2nd May 1959 showing O2 Class No.30236 waiting to leave with a train to Wadebridge. The modestly-sized town of Bodmin was remarkably well served with stations, the two main ones being Bodmin North, the former 'Southern' terminus, whilst Bodmin General was the former GWR station. In addition, of course, there was Bodmin Road on the main Plymouth to Penzance line, but this was about four miles outside the town. This historic little station depicted here, which obtained the suffix 'North' after nationalisation, had been served by O2 Class engines for many years, but 1959 was the last full year of their regular use because former GWR pannier tank locomotives took over during 1960. No.30236, which was built at Nine Elms in March 1895, remained in service for only a further seven months after this shot was taken. *DS*

Another view of Bodmin North, taken on 19th March 1966, by which time the station was very much in decline as evidenced by the lifted track. The station building seen here replaced the original Bodmin & Wadebridge Railway premises in about 1895 and there is no doubt that in its heyday this was a real gem of a station. There were several sidings and a goods shed for the handling of freight, but these were no longer required after 29th November 1965 when facilities for this traffic were withdrawn. The train is a four-wheeled diesel railbus of a type that was introduced by BR in order to reduce operating costs on lightly-used branches that were threatened with closure. It was forming a local service to Boscarne Exchange, a small halt just outside Bodmin that was constructed as late as 1964 following reductions in local train services. It enabled passengers travelling from Wadebridge to Bodmin General on the old GWR route to reach Bodmin North station and *vice versa*. *RP*

The Bodmin & Wadebridge Railway (B&WR), as previously mentioned, opened in 1834: the section from Wadebridge to Bodmin on 4th July, whilst the goods-only line to Wenford Bridge became operational from 30th September. The sharp radius curves and a very lightly laid track on the latter route proved to be the salvation for three Beattie Class 0298 2-4-0WTs which were retained solely to work the mineral trains to Wenford Bridge and outlived their sister engines by more than 60 years. This was surely one of the most delightful rural backwaters to be found anywhere in Great Britain, the use of the three well-tank locomotives only adding to its immense charm and character. The line to Wenford (as it was known locally) left the Bodmin North route at Dunmere Junction, this being the location of this shot of No.30587 pausing with the 9.35am Wadebridge to Wenford Bridge on 14th October 1960. The photographer states that the load was four vans, twenty empty china clay wagons and a brake van. He rode on the train and took morning tea with the train crew in a house near Dunmere. Happy days indeed! *JL*

Another picture of the Wenford Bridge branch, also taken on 14th October 1960, showing No.30587 shunting at the terminus after arrival from Wadebridge: this absorbing shot was taken from the steps of the overhead loading gantry. Note that, besides clay, there is also coal traffic and goods conveyed in covered wagons, though the last-mentioned are not visible in this photograph. The delightful Beattie locomotives ceased operation on the branch on 8th September 1962, after which date former GWR 1366 Class 0-6-0PTs continued to work the line for a further two years, reportedly becoming the last active BR steam engines in Cornwall. Diesel shunters then took over, continuing until 1983 when the line was, sadly, closed to all traffic. *JL*

THE GLO AND ITS PHOTOGRAPHERS

The photographs in this album were all taken by members of the GLO. This is a group of friends, some having known each other for over fifty years, who gradually got together in the 1950s and early 1960s, just by meeting on rail tours and branch lines' last day of operation.

Two enthusiasts living in the Brighton area, Gerald Daniels and Edwin Wilmshurst, became known to the writer by meeting on the 'last days' of branch lines and similar events, such as the Railway Correspondence & Travel Society's (RCTS) special trips on the Kemp Town branch in October 1952 and the closures of the Crystal Palace (High Level) line in September 1954 plus the Isle of Wight's Newport to Sandown line in February 1956. I first encountered John Britton at Gravesend (West Street) in August 1953 and again when the Kent & East Sussex Line was closed in January 1954. We were also both present when the branch from Highgate to Alexandra Palace saw its last trains in July 1954 and being members of the Ticket & Fare Collection Society (now the Transport Ticket Society) we were both anxious to obtain a selection of tickets with the date of the last day of operation stamped upon them. During 1957 we met with Chris Gammell and John Langford whilst on rail tours and on other outings, both of these gentlemen being members of the (then) Norbury Transport & Model Railway Club.

The first social get-together occurred just after Christmas 1957 at the invitation of Gerald Daniels' parents when a group of seven descended upon their home and helped to finish off the festivities. In February 1958, John Britton produced the first 'Glossary of Terms', this being a mini-dictionary of words and phrases used solely by the group on its travels and probably not understood by anyone else outside the circle. Three further editions were produced during the year. The last train on the line from East Grinstead to Lewes ran on 16th March 1958, after local people had fought a bitter battle to save their train service. The line had been closed by BR in 1955, but a local resident, the legendary Miss Bessemer, was instrumental in getting a reluctant BR to reopen the line after it was discovered that the original closure was illegal. A gathering of fourteen of us occurred at East Grinstead although at this stage a few were still unknown to the others. A compartment on the train was labelled 'Reserved for the GLO', an abbreviation coined by Chris Gammell from the 'Glossary of Terms' booklet used by the group and this was its first appearance in the public domain.

So, the GLO was born. It would be an overstatement to describe it as an 'organisation' because it has never had a constitution, committee or any officers in the normal sense. Yet despite these seeming omissions it has survived to the extent that even in retirement the group still meets each month for lunch and a drink and has an annual convention in the spring. Members keep in touch through the monthly 'GLO Circular', which, apart from a few months during 1963 when the writer worked overseas, has been produced continuously for nearly fifty years. It started more or less by accident as a single quarto sheet entitled 'Stations Closing 15th September 1958', which was just the sort of information the group needed for planning trips. Fortunately, John Stratton had access to the relevant documents at the SR Headquarters at Waterloo. From issue No.4 it became the 'GLO Circular' and around 750 editions have now been produced, with much of the input being provided by historian member Richard Maund. The format is that of an information sheet listing the openings and closures of lines/stations, including many outside the British Isles. There are also details of forthcoming GLO meetings and societies' meetings; the latter are often slide shows being given by a GLO member. Advances in technology mean that what started as a typed 'Banda' sheet producing purple ink copies, through stencils and inky fingers, to straight photocopying from a typewritten sheet, nowadays is all on computer which permits editing right up to despatch time.

When members travelled further afield (the majority worked for BR, so fares were not prohibitive!) contact was made with other enthusiasts and the membership grew to a maximum of twenty-nine. There was even a Scottish representative, the late Roy Hamilton MBE, who was a great friend and colleague to many members of the group. Four members are now aged seventy or more and still retain a keen interest in GLO activities. Sadly, two members passed away at the early age of forty-nine; they were John Phillips, some of whose pictures are included in this album, and Tom Linfoot. The GLO was 'launched', so to speak, on what is now the Bluebell Railway and the group's roots are definitely in Sussex, so it looks as though there will be some local celebration in March 2008. John Langford kindly assisted with the compilation of these notes.

Les Dench, Brighton, July 2006.

Gerald Daniels (GD), who was born in Brighton in 1938, has early memories of train spotting on post-war visits to relatives at Reading and Swansea: his first railway photographs were taken using a Box Brownie 116 camera at Feltham shed in 1953. During teenage spotting sessions on the cliff top above Brighton engine shed he met local enthusiasts Les Dench and Edwin Wilmshurst, both of whom later became founder members of the GLO. Unsurprisingly, in 1954 Gerald joined BR as a junior booking clerk. During the late 1950s branch line closures were becoming more frequent and he was kept very busy at weekends travelling the length and breadth of Great Britain (and Ireland) recording scenes on 'doomed' lines that were soon to be consigned to history. He has always been a great fan of Kodak colour film and is delighted that their products have survived the test of time so well. Gerald's railway career progressed, and after a short period in his first job he quickly moved to the (then) District Traffic Superintendent's Office at Redhill. He subsequently held posts in all three SR Divisions and in 1977 was appointed Area Manager, Surbiton. In October 1977 he organised, with the help of a colleague, a special charter train from Waterloo to Bath Spa and Oxford via the Severn Tunnel, the object being to enable participants to seek out the decent draught beer available in those cities. By this time the London area was dominated by flavourless keg beers, this no doubt being one of the reasons why the train was sold-out, a total of 596 'parched' passengers being carried. By 1982 Gerald was firmly in control of the SR's Salisbury area and spent much time trying to improve the atrocious timekeeping on the Waterloo to Exeter route which was then operated by the troublesome Class 50 diesel locomotives and plagued by delays on the long single line sections west of Salisbury. Having achieved a significant improvement in the service quality on the route, Gerald was then involved in a series of rail shows at various locations in his area. He later obtained the enthusiastic support of SR General Manager, Gordon Pettitt, for steam train rides on the Ludgershall branch and then on the main line between Salisbury and Yeovil Junction. In addition to being very profitable, these events generated enormous goodwill amongst enthusiasts and the general public. Gerald retired from BR in 1993 and is now kept busier than ever running Crookham Travel, a company specialising in day trips and longer world wide holidays for people interested in real ale, trains and trams.

Les Dench (LD), who was born in Brighton in 1935, is probably best known as one of the joint authors (with Gerald Daniels) of 'Passengers No More' (published by Ian Allan Ltd) which lists the closure date of every closed line in Great Britain. This hugely successful labour of love was first published in 1964 and was revised and reprinted twice. Les would probably prefer to be referred to as a transport enthusiast (rather than a railway enthusiast), because his interest in transport subjects includes trams, ferries and canals in addition to trains. His interest in railways developed when still at school and he fondly remembers observing Brighton locomotive shed on Saturday mornings from the cliff top in Howard Place or the end of Brighton station's Platform Two, which provided onlookers with a splendid view of movements to and from the depot. The goods-only Kemp Town branch was on his doorstep and Les recalls the RCTS 'Brighton Works Centenary' special trains from London which ran on both 5th and 19th October 1952. Local residents were offered a separate fare just for a trip on the branch and Les was immediately hooked, so much so that his quest for 'doing the track' (travelling over sections of line) has continued undiminished to the present day. He reckons to have travelled over almost all of the current National rail system, as well as several European countries and, of course, covered many lines long since closed. Les started his working life with an insurance company, but soon realised his mistake and joined BR at the end of 1953. This marked the start of a career that spanned forty years, of which two-thirds was spent on the SR in Commercial Departments at Waterloo and Wimbledon, then latterly on the ER in personnel sections. It was in the early 1960s that he took a job for six months as a 'summer relief clerk' in BR's Chicago travel office and when his posting was over he requested a fortnight's leave before returning home. After all he had accumulated his leave in North America, so why shouldn't he be allowed to take it over there! This request was granted and he set off to explore the railways of Mexico, which was, no doubt, an adventure to remember. Les took his first railway photograph in the early 1950s and started colour photography in 1960. This was, he says, a little later than some of his contemporaries, but he was still in time to record some long-forgotten scenes up and down the country.

Roy Denison (RD) grew up in Northolt, in what was then still rural Middlesex. The first railway he knew and loved was the GWR, Northolt being served by auto trains worked by pannier tank and 0-4-2T locomotives. On leaving school in 1955 Roy went to work for the Public Relations Dept. of the WR at Paddington, this being the beginning of a career that spanned forty years. Three years later he joined the Running & Maintenance Dept., working in the Shopping Control where locomotive allocation and shopping records were maintained. He was later transferred to the Trains Office at Paddington and worked in one of the old shareholders' meeting rooms which adjoined a room where some of the GWR's treasures were kept, such as Mr Brunel's portable leather cigar box which he carried with him on site visits. He says that when working alone at night in the huge office the atmosphere could be very spooky. In November 1960 Roy gained promotion to the Running & Maintenance section at Gloucester, one of his tasks being to visit various steam sheds in the area to check enginemen's route knowledge cards in order to ensure there were sufficient men available to meet traffic requirements. He remained at Gloucester until the office was closed in 1963, whereupon he was transferred to the Divisional Manager's Office at Bristol. His stay there was brief because by the end of the year he moved to the CM&EE Dept. at Paddington where he was the engine allocation clerk with responsibility for allocating locomotives to all depots throughout the WR to cover the turns allocated to them. Roy was responsible for the introduction of 14XX 0-4-2Ts to the Seaton branch (which he duly photographed, of course!) and the 64XX locomotives to the Yeovil Junction to Yeovil Town shuttle service. In 1966 he was promoted to the Locomotive Diagramming section at Paddington and later moved to the Planning Office at Euston, where he was involved in the progressive changeover from steam to diesel power. After many years working with locomotives (a series of train spotters' dream jobs one might say!) Roy became involved in a less glamorous, but equally important side of the railway, the introduction of new ticket machines. This resulted in a journey to Belfast to train staff on Northern Ireland Railways. He later became responsible for the installation and maintenance of Quick Fare ticket machines on BR. On privatisation he was given the option of remaining with a French firm that took over BR Business Systems or taking redundancy. Appropriately for somebody who had been working on Quick Fare machines he decided to make a quick getaway and left the industry in 1995. Roy took his first colour photograph in Ireland 1958, but the film was very expensive so he was unable to take as much colour as he would have liked. He does not really have a favourite class of locomotive, but prefers anything 'copper capped' or built at Swindon. His favourite line is the route from Kemble to Standish Junction, especially the section between Chalford and Stonehouse before the halts were closed.

Chris Gammell (CG), the well-known photographer, author and former publisher probably has the highest profile of any contributor to this album. He grew up at West Dulwich, near the main line from Victoria to the Kent Coast, which saw a wonderful variety of workings ranging from humble suburban electric units to gleaming BR Standard 'Britannia' Pacifics on the famous 'Golden Arrow' boat train. He became hooked on railways from an early age and, not surprisingly, joined BR on leaving school. He worked initially in the P.W. section of the Chief Civil Engineer's Office at Waterloo and was later employed on engine diagrams work in the Traffic Department on all three SR divisions. His final BR post was that of librarian at the Museum of British Transport, Clapham. One of the undoubted perks of working for BR were the very generous travel facilities available to staff of which Chris made full use, travelling widely at home and throughout many parts of Europe. His first trip overseas by rail was to Spain in 1960 and his taste for long-distance rail travel culminated in an epic journey, largely by train, to Tehran in the late 1960s. The trip took him across Turkey but Chris was unable to complete the journey by rail, being obliged to take a bus for the final stretch. This marathon was accomplished on a free ticket. In addition to trips by train across Europe and the Middle East, Chris has made visits (not on a free ticket, unfortunately) to many parts of the world to photograph steam traction, including North and South America, China, Australia, New Zealand and South Africa. His favourite country is India, however, to which he has made around ten pilgrimages, his first being in 1974. Following his departure from BR, Chris moved into publishing and worked as a publisher's representative for many years, in addition to setting up his own publishing business under the GRQ imprint. He is also an accomplished author with more than twenty titles to his credit, perhaps the best-known being his BR regional branch line series which was published by the Oxford Publishing Company. Another notable book was his 'Southern Engine Workings', which was published by OPC in 1994. This book, a publishing 'first', was full of Southern Region engine diagrams and explained the complexities of the little-known art of locomotive diagramming. Chris is well known throughout the south east of England for his entertaining talks to railway societies about past adventures. His excellent slides, coupled with his hilarious comments, usually ensure he will be asked to make a return visit. Chris took his first railway picture in about 1954, but he is no longer an active railway photographer because he does not find the current scene at all inspiring. For the record his favourite line is the St Ives branch in Cornwall, while he is a life-long admirer of the GWR 'Castle' Class.

Graham Hoare (GH) may not be the best-known contributor to this album, but he is certainly one of the most prolific photographers featured. Graham's father was a railwayman and they made many wartime journeys by train, including a trip westwards behind Lord Nelson Class 4-6-0 *Lord Collingwood*. He can vaguely remember this locomotive taking water at Salisbury and reckons it was that journey which fired his enthusiasm for the steam locomotive. After the war Graham's family took regular holidays at Bude, in Cornwall, which involved train journeys in each direction to and from Surbiton and for him the long journey was no doubt just as interesting as the holiday itself. On leaving Tiffin School, Kingston Upon Thames, Graham's father got him a job in the Permanent Way Drawing Office at Woking which started a lifelong interest in permanent way design: he subsequently worked in P.W. Drawing Offices at Waterloo, Euston, Kings Cross and Croydon. During the mid-1960s Graham was 'working' a seven-day week, earning a living in the usual way from Monday to Friday whilst enthusiastically chasing steam locomotives at weekends. Despite this hectic schedule he found time to produce a guide to Austrian Railways, which he published privately, and also wrote articles for 'Trains Annual' and 'Railway World' magazine. This was a period of great change on the railway and line closures, plus the rapid rate of withdrawal of steam traction, ensured that dedicated enthusiasts had more than enough to occupy themselves. During one year he reckons to have spent 49 out of 52 weekends chasing steam but this did not, apparently, create any domestic tension as his wife, Mary, he says, was quite content at home 'housekeeping' and 'looking after the children'. At some point Graham read Bryan Morgan's book 'The End of the Line' which encouraged him (together with the availability of free rail travel) to venture further afield across the English Channel to France, Germany, Spain and other countries where steam was still plentiful and, furthermore, maintained in good condition. The demise of steam in Great Britain prompted him to move abroad and he worked for four years in the East African Railway's P.W. Drawing Office in Nairobi. The cessation of steam there resulted in a further move to Algeria and on returning to England he was employed by a firm of consulting engineers involved in the development of the Docklands, Birmingham, and Manchester light rail schemes. Following retirement his passion for steam and travelling in general is undiminished and, he says, it has simply provided more time for him to indulge his hobby.

Roger Joanes (RJ) grew up in Bromley, Kent, and travelled to school by train. Many of the trains consisted of vintage pre-grouping coaches which had been formed into '4 SUB' electric units. Watching the trains was interesting, with plenty of steam traction passing though Bromley South in the 1950s. From the age of eleven Roger attended school with John Smallwood and they had a common interest in trains and photography. John later joined BR and this contact resulted in Roger joining the GLO. Unlike most GLO members, and certainly all those who contributed to this album, Roger did not spend his working life on the railways. He can claim, however, to have strong railway connections because, from 1972 to 1987, he lived in the former station house at Filleigh on the erstwhile Taunton to Barnstaple line. In the late 1970s/early 1980s he was involved in a campaign to reopen the Bideford to Barnstaple freight line to passenger traffic. He organised a series of charter excursion trains from Bideford to show what could be done, in addition to lobbying the politicians. The area's Member of Parliament at that time was Mr Tony Speller, who took the campaign to Parliament, and the result was his amendment to Section 56A of the Transport Act 1962 (known as the 'Speller Act'). In essence the amended Act allowed experimental re-openings. Sadly, the Bideford line closed to freight traffic before the Act could be used locally. It has, however, been employed quite extensively in other parts of Great Britain, in connection with the Bathgate and Aberdare branches and re-opened stations at Dyce and Pinhoe. Roger says his favourite lines were the Lyme Regis branch and the County Donegal Railway in Ireland. The line he most regrets having missed is the Cavan & Leitrim, also in Ireland. Today he is kept busy running 'Joanes Publications' which produces black and white transport photographs. In BR steam days Roger was primarily a black and white photographer, hence his contribution to this book appears at first sight to be modest. He scanned a number of slides, however, which ensured their appearance in the book, so his contribution is actually much more substantial than it seems.

John Langford (JL), who was born in Minehead, Somerset, in 1940 has been a railway lover for as long as he can remember. His family soon moved to Crumpsall, near Manchester, and later to Houghton-on-the-Hill, Leicestershire, before finally returning to Bexley, Kent, (where his father had remained throughout the conflict) when the threat of hostilities was thought to be over. This meant that by the time nationalisation of the railways occurred in 1948 he had lived in the territory of each of the 'Big Four' railway companies. He well remembers, as a small boy, night-time coal trains from the wharves at Erith to the gasworks of South London. His bedroom window overlooked the Dartford Loop Line and SECR C Class 0-6-0s could be heard struggling up the 1 in 100 towards Albany Park station, their exhaust beat becoming slower and slower before finally being lost in a cutting. John's father would make little drawings of ships, cranes, harbours and engines, stimulating his growing interest in transport. So, after what John says were undistinguished years at Eltham College (obviously they did not run photography classes!) and early spotting trips with a notebook and pencil, there was little doubt regarding John's chosen career. In August 1956 he joined BR, working initially at the District Traffic Superintendent's Office at Orpington. He quickly discovered that many railwaymen were also enthusiasts and he soon started attending society meetings and travelling on rail tours where he met many others who shared his passion. Free and privilege tickets facilitated travel. He particularly remembers his friendship with Cecil Chapman at (what is now called) the Norbury & South London Transport Club. John started taking colour slides (on Kodak film, of course) in March 1959 and has accumulated an extensive collection, only a fraction of which appears in this album. He has a special affection for Irish railways and was able to take colour pictures in Ireland when the fascinating railway scene there still had a real pre-grouping feel. Among favourite locomotive classes, John mentions the LSWR Adams 'Radial' and Beattie well tank locomotives and his beloved SECR C Class 0-6-0 and H Class 0-4-4T, both of which he remembers from boyhood. His varied career on BR embraced the three divisional offices of the SR, Eastleigh (Assistant Yard Master, later Assistant Station Master), Coventry, Nottingham, Birmingham New Street and Toton. Following the demise of BR (and Irish) steam in the 1960s, John found solace in the waterways of England and Ireland. Present passions are the English landscape, the life and work of Sir John Betjeman and avoiding the 'Fast Lane'. He currently lives at Long Eaton in Derbyshire.

Roy Patterson (RP) is another member of the GLO who was introduced to railways at a very early age; he was only three weeks old when he was taken on his first railway journey. Like most other GLO members he also worked on the railway, Roy's career on BR starting in the Eastbourne area (where he then lived) in 1954. He worked at various local booking offices before being called up for his national service. When this had been completed he was employed on timetable work in the operating departments at Redhill, Waterloo and East Croydon. After a short interlude in the Work Study department on the LMR at Euston he joined the WR Management Services department in 1969. He remained on the WR until retirement, mainly based at Bristol, and latterly held a post in the Training Department. Roy commenced colour photography in 1959 and mainly concentrated his interest on branch lines throughout the system which were then being closed in large numbers. He says that there were many wonderful lines around at the time, which makes it very difficult for him to nominate a favourite, but he found the group of lines around Brecon particularly attractive. Roy has photographed many locomotive classes over the years and of these he especially likes the former GWR 14XX Class 0-4-2Ts. His favourite large locomotive class would undoubtedly be Sir William Stanier's 'Princess Coronation' Pacifics. Roy now lives in retirement in the Bristol area and takes an interest in the local railway preservation scene. He also travels widely in the British Isles and Europe and sometimes further afield.

John Phillips (JP), who grew up in Beckenham, Kent, was a devoted steam man. He worked for BR and for a period was employed as a stores clerk on the South Western Division. Most of his photographic activities were on the Southern and Western Regions and he was especially fond of the Bulleid Pacifics. He covered most of the 'South Western' main lines to Weymouth and Exeter plus the various branches in Devon and Cornwall. One of his most prized shots was that of a 'Schools' Class 4-4-0 in steam long after its withdrawal from traffic: sadly, it was only *en route* to works for breaking-up. John also undertook journeys to Europe in search of steam and visited France, Belgium and Holland. Sadly, John passed away in 1989.

David Soggee (DS) has been interested in railways for as long as he can remember, but is not sure what sparked his passion for trains – there was certainly no railway background in his family. David joined BR in 1949 as an apprentice at Stratford Works and worked on steam locomotives, so he actually 'got his hands dirty' working on steam and is therefore unique among the contributors to this book. He had a 'break' when he was called up for his national service in the 1950s. In 1963 the works was closed and he found himself temporarily out of work until he got a job as a fitter with London Transport at Acton Works. Two years later he joined the SR CM&EE Dept. at London Bridge, working in the drawing office on power supply and rolling stock. The SR hierarchy decided to relocate most of the CM&EE Dept staff (who were located at various points across the region) so they would all be under 'one roof' and during the following year he was moved to Southern House, Croydon, a transfer which greatly increased the daily travelling time from his Essex home. David later worked at Liverpool Street (much more convenient for residents of Essex!) and finished his railway career with Network SouthEast, retiring in 1993. He took his first railway picture with the inevitable Box Brownie camera in 1951 during a family holiday to Budleigh Salterton, Devon, and remained loyal to monochrome until he switched to colour photography in June 1958, using an Agfa Silette 35mm. camera. He experimented briefly with other brands, but soon decided that Kodak film was by far the best. It was very expensive costing thirty-five shillings (£1.75p) for a 36 exposure roll, a lot of money at that time, but the condition of David's transparencies is just as good today as it was when the slides came back from processing, so the outlay has proved more than justified, even if it was keenly felt at the time. In 1969 David purchased an Asahi Pentax S1 camera for £100 in part exchange for his faithful Agfa Silette. He bought a Weston Master III light meter at the same time and both are still in regular use. David has always been very much a branch line photographer, especially the narrow gauge lines, and has an extensive collection of transparencies taken on Irish and European narrow gauge systems. He has concentrated almost solely on Europe, but made one long distance trip to South Africa in 1976. He particularly likes 2-6-2T engines and says his favourite standard gauge classes are the GWR 45XX plus the Gresley-designed V1 and V3 locomotives. His slide shows are always in great demand. After all, there are few photographers with top class slides of the everyday railway scene in the 1950s.

James Tawse (JT) first showed an apparent interest in railways on his way to be christened in Dundee, howling every time the train stopped. He grew up in London and soon joined the hordes of spotters at the main termini, his favourite being King's Cross, where his favourite class of locomotive, the A1 Pacifics, could also be found. In later school days, James developed an interest in railway operating and remembers getting into serious trouble after rising at 3.30am to record the progress of a succession of overnight Friday/Saturday holiday trains at Blandford Forum on the Somerset & Dorset line. This eventually led to a four-year stint with BR from 1956 to 1960, mainly at SR District Offices in the analysis and retrospective supervision of train timekeeping. It was at the Redhill office that he first made contact with the founder members of the GLO. James later moved to Canada, living there for eight years, and during this period his interests expanded to the social and historical development of railways, including those in Europe to which he made extensive trips in 1969/70. Un-typically for the GLO, his principal interest is in main line operations and in 1972 he became involved in the (then) newly formed Main Line Steam Trust at Loughborough (later Great Central Railway (1976) PLC). He purchased Bulleid 'West Country' Class Pacific No.34039 *Boscastle* from Barry scrapyard, a long story, he says, which hasn't ended yet! From the age of fifteen onwards the recording of train operation, combined with photography (he started taking colour in 1958), has been the central core of his interest, much enhanced by association with members of the GLO. Currently he is working on a long-term project with the Birmingham Central Library to formalise his collection for future use by anyone with a committed interest in railways.